SHANA,

Think Big

Complimentary
Richer Life Experience Certificate
Value $3,000

The Richer Life Connection and Rick C. Ernst invite you and one family member to attend the Richer Life Experience as complimentary guests. For more information and registration logon to:

www.MyRicherLife.com

If you **cannot** register online, call toll-free:

1-888-238-1144 ask for extension **1555***

When registering use Reference # _____

If there is no above *Reference* number simply leave blank when registering for the event.

---

* This is a *limited time offer* and all complimentary participants must attend the event by the date shown on the website:

www.MyRicherLife.com

This offer is open to all purchasers of *Richer Life Secrets by Rick C. Ernst*. Original proof of purchase is required. The above offer is limited to the Richer Life Experience only and complimentary registration for the event is subject to availability of space and/or changes to event schedule. The value of this complimentary admission for you and a companion is $3,000. To take advantage of this limited time offer you will be required to provide details of a valid credit card for a $100 deposit to secure each seat for the event registration date that you request.

If you do not attend the Richer Life Experience for the date you registered, the $100 deposit will be charged in full for each seat you registered that is not used. To avoid being charged the deposit, cancellations or rescheduling requests must be made at least five (5) business days prior to the commencement of the Richer Life Experience by calling **1-888-238-1144 ask for extension 1555**.

Corporate or organizational purchasers may not use one book to invite more than two people. While complimentary participants are responsible for their travel and other costs, admission to the Richer Life Experience is complimentary. Participants in the event are under no additional financial obligation to the Richer Life Connection or Rick C. Ernst. The Richer Life Connection reserves the right to refuse admission to or remove anyone from the premises it believes is disrupting or may disrupt the event.

Richer Life Secrets

Rick C. Ernst

MindFood
PUBLISHING

MindFood Publishing

244 Fifth Avenue, Suite 1801
New York, New York 10001-7604 USA

Scripture taken from the HOLY BIBLE, NEW INTERNATIONAL VERSION®. NIV®. Copyright© 1973, 1978, 1984 by International Bible Society. Used by permission of Zondervan. All rights reserved.

Publisher: MindFood Publishing 244 Fifth Avenue, Suite 1801 New York, New York 10001-7604 USA.

MindFood Publishing books may be purchased for educational, business or sales promotional use though special volume discounts. Please write: **Special Markets Department, MindFood Publishing 244 Fifth Avenue, Suite 1801 New York, New York 10001-7604 USA.** For more information, you may telephone: **1-800-690-4159** ask for Special Markets Department.

Throughout this book, the feminine gender is seldom referred to directly. In the interests of simplicity, the author has used gender in the generic sense in most instances with no discrimination between the sexes intended.

ISBN 978-0-615-22678-1   Manufactured in the United States of America

Library of Congress Cataloging-in-Publication Data 2008908956

Limit of Liability/Disclaimer of Warranty: While the publisher and author have used their best efforts in preparing this book, they make no representations or warranties with respect to the accuracy or completeness of the contents of this book and specifically disclaim any implied warranties of merchantability or fitness for a particular purpose. No warranty may be created or extended by sales representatives or written sales materials. The coaching and strategies contained herein may not be suitable for your situation. You should consult with a professional where appropriate. Neither the publisher nor author shall be liable for any loss of profit or any other commercial damages, including but not limited to special, incidental, consequential or other damages.

This publication is sold with the understanding that both the author Rick C. Ernst and the publisher MindFood Publishing make this book available as a success coaching publication both the author and the publisher CANNOT provide the reader with legal or financial advice. The information in this book is designed to provide accurate and authoritative information concerning the subject matter covered. It is presented with the understanding that Rick C. Ernst and/or the publisher Mind-Food Publishing is not engaged in rendering legal, accounting or other professional services. If legal advice or other professional assistance is required, the services of a competent professional person should be sought.

From a Declaration of Principles Jointly Adopted by a Committee of the American Bar Association and a Committee of Publishers and Associations.

This product is not a substitute for legal advice. *Disclaimer required by Texas statutes.*

Note From Publisher

Richer Life Secrets is masterfully written using Rick C. Ernst's unique writing style, which he has coined:

Bi-Layer Literature.

Ernst's outstanding in-depth writing approach ingeniously produces a book within a book. This allows the reader to absorb each chapter consecutively for an exciting personal growth adventure or for insightful inspirational reading, the reader may choose to focus exclusively on the bold print and remarkably receive a distinctive different version of the author's concepts, principles and success coaching.

Praise for Rick C. Ernst *and* Richer Life Secrets

"Richer life Secrets is absolutely the best collection of success thoughts and ideas ever put on paper. While reading this book, I felt as if Rick Ernst was coaching me personally. It is powerful! This and his live events are the best combination to learn how to truly live the Richer Life. It is with admiration and respect that I highly recommend you get all of Rick Ernst's coaching you can, your life will be positive affected."

Peter Mingils
CEO - PM Marketing-NetworkLeads

"Most often the first step of coaching anyone to success is to help them believe they are worthy of success and it is available to all who really want it. Rick Ernst's book does a magnificent job of both."

Ron LeGrand

"In the world today it is rare to find a person who creates success not only for themselves but for others as well - Rick Ernst is such a person. The information contained in this book is life changing!"

John E. Lang
President/CEO
Pinnacle Development Group

"Rick Ernst nailed it with this book, which gives you step-by-step coaching on how to achieve whatever you want, if it's better relationships, increased income, improved health, love or all of those. His approach has a strong Christian base with many success principles on how to quickly manifest your goals."

Rick VanWagner
Senior Pastor - Family Christian Center

Dedicated To You

As you read this book, with few exceptions you will find yourself experiencing life in one of the five categories listed below. Regardless of which station of life you currently occupy, I am confident the success principles contained within these pages will help you to reach your objectives and make all your dreams come true. Therefore, this book is dedicated to you the reader:

1. Who is just beginning to explore the possibilities, strategies and concepts necessary to experience personal growth and achievement.

2. Who is experiencing life as a robotic repetition, going to work and returning home day after day, week after week and month after month with each month running together bringing more of the same stagnant state. Your mental and emotional attitude is: "There's got to be more to life than this and I'm ready to learn how to change my situation."

3. Who has begun your journey of self-improvement and personal growth and has experienced some success but are discontent with your present pace and are now ready to pick up speed.

4. Who has overcome many challenges and possesses the character qualities and status symbols most would consider evidence of a successful life and career. However, deep down inside you feel your best is yet to come and are now seeking proven time-tested success principles that can provide you with insightful wisdom to help you reach your full potential.

5. Who at this point in your life is well down the road to success. You have experienced and accomplished more than most other people ever dream of doing. You have obtained financial independence and your focus is now on building your legacy. In so doing, you are seeking a proven blueprint to insure your time and efforts make the greatest impact possible.

My life and career have been blessed, influenced and inspired by the great writers, speakers and coaches of today and those of the past. They have helped me to learn and apply the success principles in this book and I thank God for the opportunity to share them with you.

The Richer Life:

A Consciousness Of Humility And Service To Others, In Unison With The Ongoing Pursuit Of Obtaining And Maintaining Balanced And Abundantly Fulfilled Relationships, Possessions And Esteem In Every Area Of Life.

Rick C. Ernst

Contents

Success Is Your Birthright;
Failure Is Your Option!

Rick C. Ernst

CHAPTER ONE

YOUR INFINITE RIGHT TO SUCCESS

Have you ever noticed that successful people are not always the most educated, hardest working or even the smartest individuals? Have you ever wondered why some people are successful while others are not? Have you ever asked yourself; how a successful person's thinking process is different from someone who is not successful?

The truth is successful people have discovered the secrets of success and therefore enjoy the benefits of living the Richer Life. I am excited to share with you what I have discovered to be the greatest secrets to success. Speaking of excitement, nothing is more exciting to me than the truth contained in this very first chapter: your infinite right to success. What thoughts flow through your mind when you hear these words?

You have an infinite
right to be successful.

Is this axiom true in your life? At this moment you may be, like many, full of doubt about your future. If so, set worry aside. My role in this chapter is to help you realize that every success you have ever dreamed of can be yours.

In fact, my goal is to prove to you that success rightfully belongs to you. You do have an infinite right to be successful. There is one word in that sentence that needs further explanation; that word is "infinite." I want you to know I have chosen this word very carefully.

When I say you have an infinite right, I mean you have a right that is limitless, a right that is inexhaustible. That is really the truth about your potential for success and happiness. The only limitations on success and happiness that will ever be placed on your life are those that you yourself place within your own mind.

Understand this: at this very moment, the negative cobwebs of failure and doubt can be cleaned out of your mind. At the moment you finally realize that full and lasting success is the way you were designed to live, any past failure or past mediocrity is just that—past.

Today is truly the first day of the rest of your life. At the moment you realize this, dynamic changes leading to success and prosperity will begin to take place.

This very day, positive change can begin to happen to you.

Dr. William James, the father of American psychology, stated on several occasions that people can change the direction of their lives by simply changing the direction of their thinking.

Dr. James is absolutely right.

"Action follows thought, just as night follows day."

This is a universal truth. For example, since the majority of people spend most of their time thinking about what they lack, that is, what they do not have, the result is a continuation of mediocrity.

They fail to achieve their full potential because they concentrate on what is rather than what can be.

As you observe the world around you, you will quickly perceive that while many people do live lives of mediocrity and failure, not everyone is failing. Multitudes of men and women are enjoying successful, positive, productive lives. Whenever you are ready, you can take your place as one who will be part of the continuing miracle of success. That is your potential; that is your infinite right.

If you are still not convinced, I am going to prove this point to you right now. In the school system you attended as a youngster, you were taught that the entire universe is governed by a series of laws. Everywhere in the universe, you find these laws at work. What you may not have been taught is that personal success is also regulated by law.

There is no validity in linking success to words like *luck* or *good fortune* or *getting a break* or *meeting the right person*. I might add, that is good news for you.

Success is not a matter of luck but a matter of law.

Once you understand how to utilize these laws of success, then success and prosperity will come to you. Now, no one is certain just how many success laws there may be. I personally think there may be hundreds but only a small number have been discovered to date.

Those that are known are dynamic in their ability to provide life-lasting changes for you. In this first chapter I want you to concentrate on four success laws that I will reveal to you.

I challenge you to place these laws into your life with all the intensity that you can develop. I want you to promise yourself that you will write these four laws down on a three-by-five card and carry them with you for ninety days, reading them to yourself at least three times a day. In just four weeks, you will notice a definite difference in your attitude. In sixty days, others will begin to notice the new you.

In introducing the first law to you, it is important that you understand this law is the most difficult to comprehend and to believe of the four that I will share with you.

This law may be entirely new to you. Yet this law reveals a great and marvelous truth: the thinking process of your mind which to date has created the person you are now is totally unique in nature. With that said, here is:

THE FIRST LAW OF SUCCESS:

No One Exactly Like You Has Ever Existed Before On Planet Earth.

Here is an illustration that will help you more thoroughly understand this first law. I am sure that you are aware of the value of oxygen to all life forms. Without oxygen, the earth simply does not operate. Through a basic law of nature, the plant life here on earth converts sunlight, water and carbon dioxide into sugar and oxygen. Because of this, it necessarily follows that all vegetation, even weeds, are important to our life and health.

Large groups of plants are often termed common varieties, yet they are not common at all. They are valuable assets to the planet. Without these so-called common plants, life as we know it today would cease to be.

There is a vital point here. At times you may be classified. By that, I mean you may be classified either *male* or *female*. You may even be lumped together with others, both male and female and labeled *average*. These descriptions, however, do not tell the truth about who you really are. Here is the truth:

Your mind, your thinking process, is new in nature. You have a perception of this world that no one else has ever had or ever will have.

Mark this well: you are a human being this world has never seen before. Yes, you can be classified. You are part of the human race. But once that has been said, no one has the right to put a label on you.

Even you do not know at this point what you can accomplish in the real world you live in. Your mind, your energy, is new energy and its possibilities are unlimited. You are capable of thoughts that have never been thought before.

Your age does not matter. You are a new life. You may not feel it, you may not think it, yet you are unique, different from other human beings in more ways than you are like them. You are one of a kind, an original. You are without comparison.

I can almost hear someone saying, "If all this is true, if I am this wonderful, unusual, unique person, why am I not more successful? What went wrong?" Good question. What went wrong continues to plague most people today.

You have been victimized by this world and its insistence that you live a life of conformity and develop a warped sense of consistency. More than anything else, conformity and a false quest for consistency will steal from you both the energy and creativity that makes you, you. Far too many people look as if they have been pressed out by a giant human cookie cutter.

If you are not careful, you will allow the world to mold you to its perception of what it thinks you should be rather than following your own sense of destiny. Let me state this truth as simply as I can: one of the most tragic things you can ever do in this life is to surrender your individuality, to conform to this world's human standards.

The moment you attempt to imitate another person or lifestyle, you have committed a kind of suicide. And in chasing this world's false sense of consistency, you lock up your creativity and shut down a potentially great mind.

Again, I can hear someone saying: "This all sounds so negative. Is there any hope for me?" Yes, certainly there is. If you are determined to be successful, you have to be willing to step away from the crowd. For wherever the crowd is, you will certainly find mediocrity close behind. The majority of people in the crowd have learned to be content with less than their best and that is not the life you want to live.

Here are two ideas of how to break out of the pack, away from the crowd, to release the truth of this first law into your life and to be that rare new person you were designed to be.

Determine first of all to be a whole person.

In this age of professionalism and specialization, people are often squeezed into narrow stereotypes. Many times they know much about their vocations but they do not know much about life. They are shallow breathers. Ralph Waldo Emerson foretold of this tragedy when he said:

> *"The state of society is one in which*
> *the members have suffered amputation,*
> *a good finger, a neck, a stomach,*
> *an elbow but never a whole person."*

If you are not careful, you become simply an extension of your vocation. You become a thing, a number, finally, a symbol in a computer to be maneuvered by today's electronics.

Though this is what is happening to people in ever greater numbers, it does not have to happen to you. I challenge you to:

> *Think your own thoughts.*
> *Live life on your own terms.*
> *Dare to dream lofty dreams.*
> *Be real. Let the real you come forth.*

Remember,

> *If you continue to do what you have always done,*
> *you will continue to get what you always have.*

Does that make sense to you? Of course it does. So change the quality of your thinking and you automatically change the direction of your life. Think success, live success and you will move up to success. In addition to your decision to become a whole person, follow this commitment:

> *Learn everything you can from others,*
> *but never imitate. Remember, imitation is suicide.*

When you imitate someone else, you are no longer needed. The person you are trying to be already exists. By imitating someone, you enlarge that person and diminish yourself. Remember, you are you and you are a potentially successful and prosperous person and no one—I repeat no one—will ever be quite like you. So be yourself. It is the only way you will ever reach your full potential.

> *You have a unique,*
> *literally one of a kind mind.*

You can generate dynamic new energy and the world will honor your positive thinking and action. As you put the dynamics of this first law into your life, you are preparing yourself for the climb up the ladder of success. You are reaching up with your own sense of destiny to be the star of your own choice. You are on your way!

THE SECOND LAW:

A Successful And Prosperous
Life Is Based Upon A Positive Vision
And Attitude Of Your Heart And Mind.

The most positive example of this second law is the founder of the Christian faith, Jesus Christ. He constantly urged his followers to have greater vision and look to fields that were ripe and ready for harvest. Jesus was speaking of opportunities to teach people a new way to live but his followers could not yet see what he was saying.

To Jesus, the world was ripe for a spiritual revolution. His thoughts were specific, his vision was clear and he was grounded in a positive purpose. He saw opportunities his followers would never see until they understood this second law: *a successful and prosperous life is based on the vision and attitude of your heart and mind.*

Here is how this second law works.

The present dominating thoughts of your mind mirror and color your perception of the world.

The bright rays of personal achievement, the golden hue of a successful life—it is all there for you to see and achieve according to your vision, your purpose and your commitment.

The following three ideas illustrate the value of a positive vision, purpose and commitment.

Henry Ford said:

"If you think you can do a thing or think you can't do a thing, you're right."

Yoda of *Star Wars* said:

"There is no try, only do."

King Solomon wrote:

"As a man thinketh in his heart, so is he."

Understand this: the harvest, the success and the prosperity that you gather from life are regulated by how you think, by your purpose in life, by your commitment. As strange as it sounds, the best of life goes to the person who chooses it. To say it another way:

To think is to create.

The difference between the earnings of two salespeople selling the same product for the same company may be very astronomical. One person may earn fifty thousand dollars a year, the other over five hundred thousand.

Yet in truth, both earned exactly what they saw in their minds and committed their energies. Again, to think is to create. In other words, if you can think about it, you can create it.

In Ralph Waldo Emerson's early years he served as a Protestant minister. Emerson was often criticized for speaking out against the tradition of the denomination in which he worked. To Emerson, that tradition lacked vision, purpose and commitment.

On one occasion, when a church leader said that Emerson was going to wind up in hell if he did not change his ways, another person who knew of Emerson's true vision, dedicated purpose and commitment stated, "If Emerson does go to hell, he will change the climate there and emigration will start immediately." I like that. That is how life is to be lived. You need only to capture a vision for your life and build a purpose for living. In short, get committed. With that done, you take a giant step toward success and prosperity.

When I was a child, I was taught a success proverb. A few simple words, sixteen in fact but they provide insight as to how the second law works. I challenge you to memorize these sixteen small words. Here is the proverb:

Good—better—best:
never let them rest until your
good is better and your better is best.

This simple message says whatever you do, keep your mental state supercharged with positive thoughts. Stay up mentally. It is your choice. When discouraging times come, when negative thoughts creep in, deal with them. Never give in to the mental recognition of the possibility of defeat. Positive thoughts will revive you. They will serve as a refreshing rain to a newly planted field.

Who can estimate the worth of one good positive thought? The founding fathers, the framers of the Constitution of the United States, set forth some positive thoughts, *a plan* and America was born. Henry Ford thought of the uses the common person would have for an automobile and the industrial revolution exploded.

Let me ask you an important question: is your field ripe and ready to harvest? It could be. Life, real life, success and prosperity, begin and end right in your own mind.

When you are ready for success, the world is ready for you. Build, therefore in your mind, a life of success. See yourself confident, bold and aggressive and if you do, the fruits of success and prosperity will march into your life.

THE THIRD LAW:

Every Step You Take Toward Success And Prosperity, Be It Small Or Large, Will Always Reward Itself.

This third law is a simple law but what a profound shadow it casts. To simplify the law, we could say:

Every act rewards itself.

That being true, no one has ever defined this law's value more accurately than the words of Jesus. He said:

**"Ask and it shall be given to you,
seek and you shall find,
knock and the door shall be opened unto you."**

To think positively is to act positively. To act positively is to reap positive benefits.

You can count on this third law as a fundamental truth. Success has no place for luck or breaks, only law. This law is great news. Every act of your life rewards itself. It is noteworthy that this third law of success has a built in series of checks and balances. For instance, if you attempt to seize success through negative aims, if you attempt a shortcut or try to steal another's place in line, the law is the same. You reap what you sow.

At my live events, I am often questioned about the supposed success of evil persons. It may sometimes appear that justice is blind, that evil wins and that the wicked gain. That is an illusion.

Remember this well:

The punishment is connected to crime just as reaping is connected to sowing.

Here is an example of what happens when you try to seize success through unscrupulous aims. The underworld crime figures in this country seemingly live in absolute luxury.

Yet they also live in fear. For them to move up the ladder of success in the Mob is to risk their lives, becoming increasingly distrustful of everyone, even their blood relatives.

To finally become the godfather is the one certain step to future execution or a life behind locked doors, unable to come and go out for fear of who may be waiting in the dark—or fear of arrests and long prison sentences.

It is true; you can count on it:

Every act rewards itself.

To those positive-acting people who are willing to throw themselves into the lake of life, to those who are not afraid to create ripples and waves, life gives the greater honor. That is the law and with each positive activity, be it small or great, you will be made stronger and stronger as another strand of positive energy is sent forth and ultimately braids itself into a life of success and prosperity.

THE FOURTH LAW:

You Do Not Have To Ask Others For Permission To Be Successful.

The Right To Success And Prosperity Is Infinite, Always Present, Always Near, Ever Waiting For You To Reach Out And Seize It.

Without a moment's hesitation, I can tell you that I have had few regrets in my life. Life has been exceptionally good to me. However, I do regret the hours of my young life that I spent trying to explain my vision and goals to other people. Yes, I regret my timidity to move forward.

Each year life would call me to plant and harvest a thousand acres but like so many others, I planted only a few. Like many, I ran to everyone, seeking permission to have a dream, to be visionary. Most of the time I was told to be more realistic. I started to ask a hundred times, "Do you think I could ...?" only to be interrupted by the same words: "Whatever you do, stay put." or "Do not be unrealistic."

My mistake was not in seeking to be more successful. My mistake was listening to the masses who were huddled around the fire of supposed wisdom and security. So for a time I bought the lie of my generation, as did so many of my peers, as had the generation before me. But fortunately for me I finally saw the folly in not daring to follow my own dream.

Think about your life as you read the next paragraph very carefully. What good will your retirement be if you simply rock in place, wondering what you could have been? What good is a pension if your memories are cold and damp? What good are the golden years to you if the flint was not struck, if the flame not fanned, if the success was not won, if the eternal vision was not secured?

THE FIRST PERSONAL POWER ATTRIBUTE:
Focused Energy

Once you have decided upon a specific goal, once you have put your priorities in their proper order, you will begin to sense that something is different in your life. That difference is focused energy.

This energy will not be dissipated chasing rainbows. Your eyes are now focused on your goal and each day you commit yourself to only those priorities involving your goal. With your life now focused, you have positioned yourself for success.

THE SECOND PERSONAL POWER ATTRIBUTE:
Determination

How many times have you read or heard these words: "Ladies, gentlemen, the key to success is determination. If you have that, you cannot be stopped"! That sentence is written in personal motivation books and spoken at success seminars a thousand times a day, every day of the year.

What this says about determination is true as far as it goes. The problem is that it does not go far enough. If you are to be successful, you have to be determined. The question is: where does determination come from? How do you get it? It may come as a shock to you but you do not get determination—you release it.

*A vast amount of determination is
locked inside of you at this very moment.*

It is released as soon as you establish specific goals for your life.

*Determination is a by-product
of having a specific goal, just as
gasoline is a by-product of crude oil.*

The point is no matter where you find yourself in the *now* of your life, educated or not, experienced or not, perhaps you have experienced serious setbacks. Nevertheless, think with me for a moment. In the final analysis nothing matters except this moment and this question: will you establish specific goals for your life today?

If you will, then focused energy and determination will be an integral part of your life. You will move forward. Your life will change. Success opportunities will present themselves. Memories of failure will dissolve. Visions of success will dance in your mind. Your pulse rate will quicken. Your steps will grow livelier. A certain confidence will accompany your activity. This is the fruit of specific goals. There will be a new you, a focused and determined you.

THE THIRD PERSONAL POWER ATTRIBUTE:
Enthusiasm

A recent survey reported that 85 percent of those polled stated their need for greater enthusiasm. When I read that, I thought to myself, "How did we ever stray so far from realizing the truth about enthusiasm? What happened to suggest to us that enthusiasm, so important to life and success, can be found somewhere other than inside of us?"

I have often wondered: Who betrayed the millions of men and women who hunger for greater enthusiasm? Who blinded us to the fact that, within each human being, our creator has placed all of the enthusiasm one will ever need for laughter, for the good life, for prosperity?

I do not know how we became so confused but the lie continues. People spend entire lifetimes and exceptional amounts of money in an attempt to become "more enthusiastic," to learn how to live an excited life.

Yet enthusiasm this fire, this bold streak that fills up a life with excitement for success, cannot be bargained for or purchased.

I promise you that enthusiasm, like focused energy and determination, will rush into your life once you have established specific goals.

THE FOURTH PERSONAL POWER ATTRIBUTE:
Courage

The courageous are always in the minority. Yet they are the honored, the revered, the imitated and the successful.

Aristotle said:

> *"I count him braver who overcomes his*
> *desires than him who conquers his enemies,*
> *for the hardest victory is the victory over self."*

Aristotle knew that it is through the act of goal setting that you put yourself in charge of your life. Goal setting puts focused energy, determination, enthusiasm and self-control, which is courage, into your life. Once you have all four of these attributes in abundance, they will aid you in your success journey.

THE FIFTH PERSONAL POWER ATTRIBUTE:
Specific Action

Ralph Waldo Emerson was right on target when he stated:

> **"The ancestor of every act is thought."**

To think is to act. That's right. To think is to act. In addition, setting specific goals is the highest form of success thinking in which you can engage. Setting specific goals will produce specific actions. Thomas Huxley once wrote:

> *"The great end of life is not knowledge but action."*

You must decide once and for all, what you want out of life and then clearly define those desires and wants, crystallizing them into specific goals. Then you will discover that success and prosperity are on the way. Think of the renewed strength and vitality you will have when you possess focused energy, determination, enthusiasm, courage and specific action, the ability to act decisively and quickly. Your personal success is assured as you develop the art of setting and reaching specific goals.

Now here is a proven action plan for the process of setting and reaching specific goals. I have used this success plan for years. It has worked for me and it will work for you. There are twelve exciting, fun-filled steps you must complete in setting your action plan in order. Prior to sharing this action plan with you, I have two admonitions I want you to consider, both of which are very important.

One: once you begin to set specific goals, you may find yourself going against the grain of the kind of security your family and friends have decided is best for you.

People will react differently to you when you announce that you are turning over a new leaf in your life. Some will be supportive, of course but others will feel a need to tell you to be more realistic about your expectations. My coaching is to be kind to everyone who questions your new life but remember it is *your life.* Do not wake up at age sixty-five wondering what you could have been. Goal setting allows you to become the man or woman of your dreams, to be a whole, happy person.

Two: When people begin to set goals, they usually place a great emphasis upon their financial goals, upon wealth, property and the like.

I understand that motivation. Dreams do have to be funded. The point I want you to consider is this: there is more to your life than finances, more than just making money. There are eight areas of your life wherein you should set one or more specific goals: *spiritual, family, vocational, financial, physical, social, mental and long-term.* After you have your goals set in each of these eight areas, you are on your way to exciting success. Then you will realize the truth of Emerson's idea:

> ### *"The world makes way for*
> ### *the person who knows where he's going."*

Now to the twelve secret steps to setting and reaching specific goals.

Step number one: ***To begin the quest of setting and reaching specific goals, you must concentrate on answering the following three questions:***

One: What do I want to do with my life?

Two: What do I want to have from life?

Three: What do I want to become over my lifetime?

Answering these three questions fully, honestly and completely is not only the first step but also the most important step. At that very moment you decide what you are going to do with your life. This is the time to get serious about the direction of your life.

> ### *What do you want to do with your life?*
> ### *What do you want to have?*
> ### *What do you want to become?*

When you can answer these three questions, you are 90 percent of the way to the wonderful world of success and prosperity. Even though there are eleven other steps in this goal-setting strategy, this first step cannot be sidetracked or minimized.

This single success activity will set the direction for all the rest. When you answer these three questions, you have begun your journey to the stars. The answers to these three questions are in fact, the turning point in your life. These questions are simple to state and easy to repeat. However, when the answers take root in your life, you are on your way. So take your time, think it over and let your mind soar. Dare to dream a lofty dream. Dare to see yourself as a full and complete success. Remember:

To think is to create.

Step number two: ***Involve members of your family or business in the goal-setting process.***

It is a wise decision to involve everyone who should be involved.

Step number three: ***Decide why the goals you have chosen are important to you.***

Decide exactly what personal motive and rewards are behind these goals. This is a far more important step than you might realize. Here is why: you would be very surprised if you knew how many people are out there in life chasing dreams that are not their own. It shocks me to realize just how few people truly stand on their own, dream their own dreams and march to their own drumbeat. I am counting on you to be one who does.

Getting wise counsel from successful and experienced people is always the right thing to do. But the bottom line is you must decide what goals are right for you. It is your life.

Step number four: ***Always reduce your goals to clearly defined written statements.***

The object is to crystallize your dreams by writing out each of your goals. This is one of the most exciting parts of the twelve steps. In some ways, this is a difficult step. It is decision time: the moment you are going to take the wraps off your life, the moment you set in motion your entire future. As you write out your goals be specific. Words such as *maybe, hope to, someday* and *try* are never to be used. Be specific. Words such as *will, reached, completed* and *now* are words of a successful person.

Step number five: ***Establish official starting dates for all of your goals.***

Until you decide a definite time to begin a committed effort your goals remain only wants, wishes and maybes. Being specific about your life is more than toying around with a dream or two. It is establishing start dates for each goal and then launching the effort with total commitment.

Every race has a starting line. If you are going to be in the race, you have to enter, appear and start. All this is a prelude to the possibility of winning. So it is in the race of life. You must enter, appear and start. That, frankly, is most people's problem. They are always preparing to live but never seem to get beyond the preparation step.

I challenge you to set those starting dates and start on time in launching your effort. I would rather aim at the stars and end up at the top of the mountain than wander around in the valley of life simply carrying my entry blank.

Step number six: ***Establish official completion dates for all of your goals.***

It is not only important to begin; it is even more important to finish. The saying is true: any horse can start a race but only thoroughbreds finish. Life is a serious business. There is no on-the-job training for life. You get one shot at it. You have to make the most of it.

The person who said, "It does not matter whether you win or lose, it's how you play the game" was talking about a game. He was not talking about life. If he were, he would be grossly mistaken. When you think about success remember what the great football coach Vince Lombardi said:

> ***"Winning isn't everything.***
> ***It's the only thing."***

In the business of success, there are only winners and losers. There are those who did not start and did not finish; there are also those who started but did not finish; and then there are those few who started and finished. Make up your mind at this very moment. You are not only starting toward success, you are also going to finish. So establish those completion dates.

Step number seven: **Read your goals to yourself at least three times a day.**

It will take less than ten minutes a day to read your goals to yourself. The object is to burn your goals into your memory. Not only is this a good exercise to stimulate and program your subconscious mind, but it is also one of the best ways to gain new ideas and insights as to how to reach your goals.

Step number eight: **Do not reveal your goals to anyone who will react negatively.**

Of all the twelve dynamic steps in the goal-setting process, this *must never be violated*. Again, do not reveal your goals to anyone and I mean anyone, who will react negatively.

This may mean that sometimes you will have to keep your goals completely to yourself. Whatever it means, you must do it. We are talking about your life and you cannot afford the luxury of negative friends or associates.

Discover those people who are interested in talking about positive ideas, those who are serious about success and those who see that life is an adventurous journey.

> **Make a determination to be**
> **positive, to stay positive and to**
> **associate with others who are also positive.**

Step number nine: **Pray about your goals.**

This is the simplest concept of all, at least for me, to write about. Make your goals a part of your prayer life. Not only will this aid you in making your prayer time more exciting but also when you success-fully reach each of your goals your faith will be strengthened.

Step number ten: **Believe your goals will happen.**

The tremendous importance of believing in yourself and your goals can be best understood in a comment of John Adams, the second president of the United States:

> **The real American Revolution occurred
> first in the minds and hearts
> of the American people.**
>
> **The American people believed it was time for
> a change and once that goal was established and
> believed, the American Colonies became undefeatable.**

Adams was right. Belief must take up residence in both your heart and your mind.

In your heart, *belief* is spelled *T-R-U-S-T*.

- **Trust in your creator.**

- **Trust in yourself.**

- **Trust in your ability.**

- **Trust in the laws of success to work for you.**

In your heart belief is spelled, *T-R-U-S-T*. In your mind belief is spelled, *Y-E-S*. Say yes to today. Say yes to your goals. Say yes to your plans. Say yes to your success!

Step number eleven: **Set aside at least five minutes each day for mental goal visualization.**

Simply closing your eyes and seeing yourself on the screen in your mind in full possession of all your goals. Believe me; this habit will pay rich dividends.

Specialists who concentrate their efforts in understanding how the mind works have known for a long time of the two basic compartments of the mind: the conscious and the subconscious.

It is in the subconscious mind that the future direction of your life begins to take place. Once the subconscious mind understands exactly what you want to do, to have and to become, it will direct your total energies to see that these goals are achieved.

Investing at least five minutes each day with your eyes closed, seeing yourself in possession of all your goals, will serve as a compass for your mind. You will be pointed in the success direction.

Step number twelve: ***Live your life with positive expectancy.***

Why not? At this point you have your goals clearly set. You have every right to get up in the morning expecting the rising sun to be there just for you. You are on purpose. You have every right to expect the laws of nature to wrap around you and carry you above the mundane, hesitant, negative majority. As a goal setter, you are in sync with every known law of success.

You are moving with the flow of positive energies. You are on your way up to success. Yes, it is your turn now, so live each day with positive expectancy. I often hear people say, "I wish I were a more powerful type of person, more dynamic." I have good news. Everyone can have more *personal power*.

How? There is a simple secret to *personal power*.

Here is the secret:

Balance is the key to personal power.

That is why these next few weeks are crucial for you. Determine to establish at least one goal for every area of your life.

James Allen wrote:

"Dream lofty dreams,
for the vision you hold in your
heart will one day become reality."

Remember what Emerson said:

"Hitch your wagon to a star."

So look up! Catch your own personal star! Go for it! It is there for you today. Do not wait! Start now; with your goals clearly set in every area of your life, you are primed for success!

*Believing Is The Acceptance
Of A Fact That Cannot Be Proven
Or Demonstrated By The Process
of Logical Thought.*

Rick C. Ernst

CHAPTER THREE

BELIEVING MAKES IT HAPPEN

One thing is demonstrated each day in the world we live in, success and prosperity is being achieved all around us. Nothing is more common in America than failures becoming successful, losers becoming winners, the poor becoming rich and those who have been overcome becoming over comers.

There is one seemingly miraculous event after another, yet we should not be surprised by this. All these wonderful success stories have one common ingredient:

Believing makes it happen.

The fact that you are reading this book leads me to believe that you truly want to learn the secrets of success and move forward to the bright and glorious new day of prosperity. That is exactly what I want for you, too. I am not in this business primarily for profit or fame. That will not satisfy me. I will be satisfied only if I can provide you with the answers you seek.

In this chapter, I will give you another startling success secret to aid you in your quest for living the *Richer Life*. The secret is; *believing makes it happen.*

Thus far, I have provided you two great secrets of success. One, you do have an infinite right to be successful, a right no one can take from you. As long as you live, it is yours. Two, setting specific goals for your life develops a vision, a mindset for success that will not go away until you have become the person of your dreams.

In this chapter you will discover the power and pleasure of faith.

So many people live their lives with the attitude of lack rather than the rule of faith.

They think good things happen but only to others, never to them. Because they have little or no belief in themselves, their goals or their dreams, they often trade it all away for supposed security by training for a vocation and lifestyle they will finally come to hate.

Some work all their lives for a major corporation only to watch their supposed security trampled upon by corporate raiders, mismanagement by leadership or the tumbling of the economy into recession or depression, causing their industry to lay off, cut back or even fail.

When you fully understand the dynamics of this third secret, believing makes it happen; you will never again feel as if you have to let someone else usurp your dreams. You will never again have to feel trapped. You will be able to live life at the crest of success, not in the valley of despair.

You may be saying to yourself, "All this sounds well and good but what is *believing* anyway?

- *What do I have to do?*

- *How will I know if I have faith?*

- *How does it work?"*

Good questions, all of them; in this chapter I will answer each of them clearly and fully.

First, let us start with a definition of believing:

Believing is the acceptance
of a fact that cannot be proven or
demonstrated by the process of logical thought.

For instance, Wilbur and Orville Wright built a machine that came to be known as an airplane. It was first a machine of faith, their personal faith, because many wise men of their day ridiculed them.

However, the Wright brothers accepted as fact that somehow man could fly something that had not been proven or demonstrated with logical thought. Once that machine left the ground, it was no longer a machine of faith but a machine of empiricism, a science that reasons from observation.

Empiricism believes
after it happens;
faith believes before it happens.

The world is full of people who say after an event takes place, "I knew it could happen; I knew it." Rarer is the person who before the event says, "I know it can be done and I'm going to do it."

I want to expound on the case for developing a strong personal belief system in you, in your aspirations and goals. Here is what others have said about believing and about having faith.

John Stuart Mill said:

"One person with belief
is equal to a force of
ninety-nine who have only interests."

Dr. William James said:

"Believe that life is worth living,
and your belief
will help create the fact."

Napoleon Hill said:

*"Whatever the mind of man can
conceive and believe, it can achieve."*

Count Leo Tolstoy said:

"Faith is the force of life."

Charles Kingsley said:

*"I do not want merely to possess a faith;
I want a faith that possesses me."*

Jesus said:

"Fear not only believe..."

I trust these ideas will lodge deep within your heart and mind. All successful people operate in the realm of faith. This world was designed so that you could fully develop your faith and in so doing be successful and prosperous. Faith, to believe in one's creator, oneself, one's goals, is the key source of power for success.

By this exercise, that is, the use of your faith, it grows and becomes a powerful tool for achieving victory in every area of life.

You may be asking the question, "If faith is so important, so vital for my success, why is it so rare? Why do most people speak only of being realistic or of not taking chances, of not daring to dream the big dream?" Ah, you put your finger on a major problem.

For everyone who believes, there are 10,000 doubters. These doubters may be in your own household. They are often found among those closest to you—parents, spouses, relatives, friends, teachers, employers and even the clergy.

Doubting is easier than believing. It is the broad road. And many walk thereon. In believing, however, there is power. Your eyes will be opened, your opportunities will become plain and your vision will become reality.

The fact is that both doubting and believing are learned reflexes. I can teach you four dynamic ideas to increase your faith, thus eliminating from your life those lingering doubts that have kept many from the full success for which they have been searching.

IDEA NUMBER ONE:

The Weight And Power Of Your Faith Will Always Be In Direct Proportion To The Clarity Of Your Goals.

The formula is simple: dynamic vision and crystal-clear goals equal explosive and permanent faith. The by-products of this faith will be virtuous character. Among those virtues will be courage, strength, honesty, conviction, loyalty and endurance as well as enthusiasm and love for life. Robert Collier said:

> *"Your belief that you can do the thing gives your thought forces their power."*

Mark this down, vision plus clarity of goals, releases faith that extends itself into your life and keeps you moving forward toward the success and prosperity you desire. By the very act of establishing goals for your life, by designing in your mind and writing down your personal aspirations for success, you unlock the dynamic power of faith. To have faith or to believe in yourself and your goals is to tap into an eternal truth, to live as the truly *great* lived. Here is an insightful sentence from the book of Hebrews 11:1. Read it carefully and you will see more clearly the dynamics you have tapped into.

> *Now faith is being sure*
> *of what we hope for and*
> *certain of what we do not see.*

There it is. The faith, the belief, which is released in the setting of specific goals, will provide for you a certainty that all your hopes and dreams will come true. You can be absolutely sure that one day you will have in reality those things that are now only present in your mind. It is absolutely true:

To think is to create.

Yes believing makes it happen and the possession of specific, clear, concrete goals, gives faith its focal point. From there your faith will spread into all of your being. You will see the impossible. You will feel the impossible. You will achieve the impossible. It is true; *believing makes it happen.*

Jesus, the master teacher in the land of Galilee some two thousand years ago, was one day found stressing the value of faith. He absolutely understood that even a tiny faith was explosive. He knew the uniqueness of faith as no man before him or after him. Jesus said, "I tell you a truth: if you have faith as small as a mustard seed, you can say to this mountain, 'move from here to there,' and it will move. Nothing will be impossible for you." Faith once released and held firmly, will multiply itself.

The result is that you see what others cannot see. You are invincible. You understand the meaning behind Napoleon's declaration:

"Impossible is not a French word."

You know that all things are possible for you. Success and prosperity is a way of your life, not by chance but by choice. So my challenge to you is to constantly refine your goals. Know what you want and why you want it. As you do these basic things, faith will be present. Your success will be assured. You will experience for yourself:

To think is to create.

IDEA NUMBER TWO:
Determine To Live Your Life In The Present, Not The Past, While Planning For The Future.

You must accept the fact that the past lives in you but you do not have to live in the past. If you search through the centuries for wisdom concerning the good life, the life of success, you will discover that the true leaders understood the value of learning from the past, living in the present and planning for the future.

If the life you lived in the past was not satisfactory, was not full and rewarding, why would you want to keep thinking about it, holding onto it? If you live in the past, it is surely a prison and the guards have blindfolded you so that you cannot see the horizon. When you decide to live in the present—and it is a decision no one else can make for you—it is as if the great judge of life has granted you a pardon. You are released from your old life to think new thoughts, to see yourself as a new person.

The value of thinking new goal-directed, success-motivated thoughts cannot be overstated.

Listen to this advice from five world-renowned teachers.

Dr. Joyce Brothers:

> **"Success is a state of mind, if you want success; start thinking of yourself as a success."**

Orison Marden:

> **"What we sincerely believe regarding ourselves is true for us."**

Claude Bristol:

> **"What you believe yourself to be, you are."**

James Allen:

> **"A man is literally what he thinks."**

Anton Chekhov:

> **"Man is what he believes."**

These people were all echoing one single theme: believing makes it happen. You cannot have a life of true success without a heart full of faith. What you believe, whatever your faith is or lack of it, controls your future. Without question, one of the modern twentieth century giants of success, fame and fortune is Richard M. DeVos, one of the two partners who began the giant Amway Corporation. DeVos has an idea that I truly appreciate:

> *"The only thing that*
> *stands between a man and what he*
> *wants from life is often merely the will to*
> *try it and the faith to believe that it is possible."*

Now that is valuable information. The object is to keep moving forward, to advance toward the completion of your goals and dreams. Looking back, living in the past, hinders you and slows you down. You run the risk of getting negative about life. In so doing you use success energy foolishly.

This is the reason Jesus, who is the source of all wisdom made this dramatic statement: "No man, having once put his hand to the plow, looking back, is fit for the kingdom." Jesus is saying you can look in only one direction at a time.

You can think only one thought at a time. You have to make up your mind. You must force yourself to learn from the past, live in the present and plan for the future.

Once you decide to do that, you will settle for nothing less than success. From this moment on, I encourage you to be on guard. Place a sentry at the door of your heart and determine that not one word of negativity will be allowed to pass.

Now that you know the secret, look at your mind for a moment as a container that can hold water. If you wanted to get the water out of the container and you were not allowed to tip it over, one thing you could do is to put rocks in the container to raise the water level.

Chapter Four

THE ART OF SELF-RELIANCE

A t this point we will begin a very unusual study together. I am indebted to Ralph Waldo Emerson for some of the ideas in this chapter. Emerson was among America's first and most dynamic example and teacher of the art of self-reliance.

This much is clear, when you understand the laws of success as I have outlined them for you in Chapter One regarding your infinite right to be successful. Chapter Two's ideas of how to get your life more focused and specific. Chapter Three's principles of building faith, you learned that believing makes it happen.

In so doing, you are on course to becoming a self-reliant person, the greatest personal gift you can ever give yourself. Then your success will be assured, peace and personal security won.

When I use the word *self-reliant*, do not become confused as some do, in misrepresenting what Emerson and others are saying. I am not saying that as a self-reliant person you can do everything.

As a follower of the Christian way, I have come to understand that I can accomplish very little without God's help.

However, I have also learned that whatever I find myself engaged in, I should give it my best. Therefore, I look at each day with the understanding that I am given twenty-four hours of unblemished opportunity and it should not be wasted. I will rise up and move forward to the completion of my goals. I will ask no favor, nor expect any. I will misuse no man, nor allow myself to be pushed aside.

This is the spirit of self-reliance, of assurance, the victory of which I speak. Self-reliance is a boldness for life. Self-reliance is the courage to pursue excellence and never to be satisfied with less than your best.

Self-reliance is actually a way to express the gift of personal power that your creator has given you. Power until now, may have lain dormant in your life. This newfound personal power cultivated will lift you to new and exciting levels of achievement. When I use such a word as *power* and suggest that you possess *personal power*, the term itself can be confusing for many. You may be saying, "Power? I do not feel very powerful. If self-reliance is personal power, then I am a long way from having self-reliance in my life."

I understand your feeling. I have been where you are. However, let me assure you that you are far closer to being a self-reliant person than you may think. Self-reliance is your destiny. It will happen.

In just a moment, I am going to share with you four axioms and absolute truths related to self-reliance. I am going to insist that you take these four dynamic truths and memorize them. Wear these truths as a shield, for at times, life can be rough and as Emerson states, "will swallow your ship as a grain of dust." Life is real. It is combat. Winners win and losers lose. It is by developing the self-reliant life that you forge your own destiny, create your own success and capture your own star.

I challenge you to read this chapter repeatedly, until these four axioms are burned into your subconscious. This commitment will lead you to dynamic new thoughts about yourself and your future. Perfection regarding self-reliance will not arrive in your life overnight but you will develop new attitudes about yourself and you will know that success is in your future. You will be changed and you will definitely like the new you.

Follow these four axioms and you are on your way to prosperity.

THE FIRST AXIOM OF SELF-RELIANCE:

To Dream Your Own Dream,
To Seek Your Own Destiny,
To Acquire The Success You Desire.

These Are Infinite Rights
Given To You By Your Creator.

This axiom represents a giant step forward in acquiring self-reliance. It declares that your first waking thought as well as your last thought for the day should be; *God has made me a very special person.* In fact, I am unique, one of a kind. I am designed for success. I am determined not to let anyone or anything steal success from me.

I am developing a vision for my life. I will be specific. I will throw off my old ways, old thoughts and habits that have held me back. I will dream my own dream and move forward to possess it. This is the mindset of a self-reliant person.

Let me ask you a question. Who are the people in this life who have become excitedly successful? Are they lucky? Are they gifted? No! A thousand times no!

Success begins when you finally throw off all the negative thoughts and yes, even lies, that you have told yourself as to why you are not already a success.

To put it another way, like all who have achieved success, you must take control of your thoughts. New thoughts must overcome old thoughts. Positive ideas must overcome negative ideas. Faith must overcome fear.

These counter and opposite views will fight for the dominant role in your life but you hold the final decision. No one can make you think a thought you do not want to think or live a life you do not want to live. Until now you may have been doing so but that is all going to change.

You are now going to assume control of your destiny in life by taking control of your thoughts. The words *can't, might* and *maybe* will be replaced with *can, will* and *sure*. The bottom line is:

The real battle for success takes place in the mind.

Here is a suggestion that will keep you on target. Actually, it is a reading list. If you are truly serious about success, I want you to commit yourself to reading seven books over the next six months. I guarantee these books will be a life-changing force for you. These seven books will fill your mind with hundreds of positive, dynamic concepts about life, peace of mind and success—your success. I have chosen these seven books for two very sound reasons.

One, these seven books are the best success motivation volumes ever written. Two, not one of the seven was written with a financial profit motive. To be blunt, much of today's personal achievement material is simply trash or a shallow rehash of partial truths packaged to attract, promising everything and delivering little.

What I am suggesting you read is classic success achievement material. It does not get any better than these books. Here are the seven books; I also think it best if you read them in the order in which they appear.

One: James Allen's little book, an essay, *As A Man Thinketh.*

Two: The Gospel According To *John*

Three: The Gospel According To *Matthew*

Four: Ralph Waldo Emerson's essay *Self-Reliance*

Five: Emerson's essay *Compensation*

Six: The Book of *Psalms* from the *Old Testament*

Seven: Again from the *Old Testament*, the Book of *Proverbs*

It will take you some time to read and study thoroughly this marvelous material but believe me; it will be to your advantage. Your mind will be rewarded with absolute truths about life, success, prosperity, peace and eternity.

These truths will serve as a weapon to be used against the challenges of life that come against all of us. In the final analysis, *nothing matters except the thoughts of your own mind.*

You can give your life over to flimflam, to worldly reasoning; you can allow negativity to chain you to the masses who have accepted mediocrity as a way of life. On the other hand, you can give your mind to the superior thoughts of time and eternity. You can catch the freedom train right inside your own mind and ride it to success. Ultimately, the decision is yours.

The competing forces of negative and positive will pull and tug at the very core of your mind but at any moment, you can decide the direction your life will pursue.

Today life has smiled on you. You are alive. You are breathing. You are listening to someone who wants the best for you, someone who knows what it is to struggle and eventually win.

See in your mind's eye Allen, John, Matthew, Emerson, David, Solomon, Jesus; see them all at the crest of the hill waiting for you. It is your turn to walk on Success Avenue.

Your destiny is to achieve success. To realize this is to throw off the restraints, to come out of the shadows of doubt and despair into the sunlit fields of perseverance, promise and the prosperity of living as a self-reliant person. Now let us move to the second axiom:

THE SECOND AXIOM OF SELF-RELIANCE:

Between The Beginning And The End Of Your Success, You Can Expect Setbacks And Struggle, Yet If You Continue, You Will Succeed.

Until That Day Arrives, Carry Yourself With Dignity And Determine To Live Self-Reliantly.

My comments on this great truth will be brief. Yet do not allow my brevity to overshadow the profound truth of this second axiom. In life bad things sometimes happen. In the quest for success, setbacks are commonplace.

There are many stories of men and women who, in the process of becoming successful, failed miserably. Many suffered extensive losses, even bankruptcy. Yet they continued on; they persevered and finally won the victory. No matter where you are now, on the bottom struggling, experiencing severe setbacks, this is my coaching: straighten up, stand tall and carry yourself with dignity even if you are penniless.

Remember this:

Being broke is only temporary;
being poor is a state of mind.

If you are not doing as well in life as you would like, so what? You can turn it around. Walk in accordance with the great truths you now know. Never let your emotions rule your life. I do not know how it came about, that you have this book. Maybe someone gave it to you. Or maybe you heard me speak at a live event and purchased it afterward or heard me on the radio. Perhaps you responded from our TV infomercial. Whichever it was, obviously you must have been touched by one or more of my ideas and impressed enough to want to purchase it. When I say impressed, I am assuming you thought I am successful and could help you improve yourself as well. If this was your thought, you are right. By God's grace, my life has been super-blessed, including many of the material and financial privileges people think of when they define success.

However, I also know what it is like to struggle, to not have enough money and to fall flat on my face while trying to do my best. I have had a lot of deals go bad. I have owned many companies that have gone out of business. Some never even got off the ground for one reason or another. I have tried many, many times in a lot of different ways to become *successful*. In fact, I have had many more so-called failures than successes. After it all, this I know for sure:

> *If you are going to succeed,*
> *you are going to have setbacks,*
> *disappointments and hard times.*

The good news is success is available to those who *do not quit*. All of your dreams, just like mine, can come true but you must first imagine the dream fulfilled. It is your turn now! Go for it. Do it!

Remember:

> *To think is to create.*

THE THIRD AXIOM OF SELF-RELIANCE:
Never Envy Or Covet Another's Position In Life.

You must understand that envy is ignorance. Set forth on your own personal success journey, *not someone else's plan*, learning from both victory and failure. In the process you will slowly but surely develop a strong spirit of self-reliance. Emerson's brilliant essay on self-reliance develops several dynamic ideas, gems of reality for you to consider. He writes:

> *There is a time in every man's education when*
> *he arrives at the conviction that envy is ig-*
> *norance; that imitation is suicide; that he*
> *must take himself for better, for worse, for his*

> *portion; that though the wide universe is full*
> *of good, no kernel of nourishing corn can*
> *come to him but through his toil bestowed*
> *upon that plot of ground which is given him*
> *to till.*

Emerson lived in the early and middle 1800's. His illustrations were drawn from nature, not technology. Yet his points about self-reliance are crystal clear. In fact Emerson makes four points in this one small paragraph. If you are committed to living as a self-reliant person, these four ideas may be just the success information you need.

First, Emerson says that envy is ignorance and he is exactly right. To covet what someone else has harvested is a fruitless exercise. Success is yours if you claim it. There are no shortcuts. Success is a straight line from where you are to where you want to be.

Here is a great clue to the wisdom of Emerson's statement. Do not see things as they are; see them as you want them to be. Press forward and keep your specific goals, dreams and ambitions before you. Success will happen to you.

Second, Emerson says that imitation is suicide. Again, he is right. The answer is to not mind what others think. *Mind what you think.* When all is said and done, you are going to have to live with the life you are building. So do not be jerked here and there by society.

Think for yourself. Act for yourself. Do what you need to do. Insist on being yourself and the world will be a better place because you lived. Blossom where you find yourself planted. At every turn seek the high ground, no matter how difficult. Go the extra mile. Do unto others as you would have them do unto you.

Honor the success of others, learn from them but never, never imitate. You are equal to all men. Your potential for success is truly great. We do not all start in life at the same level, yet life honors every positive step and your reward for persevering will be self-reliance.

Third, Emerson says you must learn to accept yourself right where you are in the *now* of your life. That is a great admonition and one worthy of consideration. However to accept yourself is not the same as being satisfied with yourself.

The Apostle Paul, the great Christian teacher, writing to those of the Christian faith, stated, "In whatever condition I find myself, I am content." Yes, self-acceptance and contentment are great virtues but never, I repeat, never be satisfied. There is always a way to do a thing better, always a way for greater achievement in both your personal life and your work in the world around you.

Too many people attempt to build around themselves a comfort zone, a cocoon and there they remain. In a sense they think they are protected from the risks of life. They are protected, yes but at the same time they are destined to mediocrity, never to feel the triumph of victory over self, of going beyond the norm, of stretching to new dimensions of achievement. We are all called to be beautiful butterflies, to break out of cocoons that have imprisoned us and kept us from knowing the full strength and dynamics of self-reliance. To be a self-reliant, success-driven achiever is to be born again in the human sense of life. Richard Evans said:

"Everyone who has gotten where he is had to begin where he was."

Does that statement register with you? No one really has any other choice. You are where you are. You can lament that fact if you wish but it will not change anything. Fretting, wishing, moaning and groaning are not the answer.

Accept your starting point; you cannot change it. However, you can start anew where you are. Let that dissatisfaction in your heart come forth as positive energy, as a faith that believes in your infinite right to be successful. Let that energy create in you a need to focus on the accomplishments of your goals and ambitions. Then your life will take a turn for the better. That is a solemn promise from me to you.

Fourth, Emerson says, "there is as much to learn from failure as from success." It seems to me the greatest tragedy of life is not that a person fails but that they have *failed to attempt* to become the man or woman of their dreams.

Here is a law of life:

Power ceases in the instant of repose

It is a strange truth but true nevertheless. You lose no personal power in failing. Obviously you lose none when you are successful. It is when you fail to attempt that you suffer your greatest loss. "Power ceases in the instant of repose." Or to state it another way, more will be lost by indecision than by wrong decision.

The key then to being successful is to stay active. If one plan does not work out, go to plans B, C, D and so on. Stay at it! Keep focused. Every act rewards itself. Some of life's greatest successes, like Thomas Edison the inventor and Louis Pasteur a great scientist, to name just two, were familiar with failure, setback and loss. Yet they remained focused, their vision clear. They kept on keeping on, learning from every difficult situation until failure turned to success. The same spirit that abides in them abides in you. Use it and self-reliance is yours. Here is the fourth and final axiom:

THE FOURTH AXIOM OF SELF-RELIANCE:
Conformity Is A Plague
Within The Human Consciousness.

It is a slow but certain form of suicide. Living as a self-reliant person means being a nonconformist in every area of your life. Emerson was very blunt when he wrote, "If you're going to be a man, you will be a nonconformist." I want you to look at what a nonconformist is and how by becoming a nonconformist you authenticate your true humanity and express your individuality, actually ensuring your best hope for success. First, let it be clear that not *all* conformity is bad. Society, for instance, is based on laws and standards to which we voluntarily conform thus establishing a community wherein we can live in peace without fear of hostile aggression against our person. Conforming to standards of law and order is a good kind of conforming.

Webster's dictionary describes conformity as *likeness in shape, design and form*. It is compliance. Here is the dark side of the definition of conformity. *It is conforming to an accepted practice or standard*. Underline in your mind the word *accepted*. Accepted practices are usually practices created by the majority, the masses, those who would control. Just because something has been accepted as a standard does not make it right.

Hitler taught that extinguishing Jews, even Jewish children, was right. It became an accepted practice. Even those who thought it wrong often went along. They conformed. Over six million Jews lost their lives.

In the United States in the 1800's an accepted practice in the South was that rural and mundane labor was handled by slaves. Did that make slavery right, just because the powerful, southern majority accepted it? These two illustrations cause emotions to rise. I trust it is that way with you.

Accepted practices and standards are fine in many ways but when conformity steals from you, life, liberty and the pursuit of excellence, you need to take a long look at the direction conformity is taking you. If you allow yourself to be led by others, life is sure to be dismal and bland. For sure there is risk in being your own person. However, there are also great rewards.

When you were born you were given a name. Chances are that other people living or deceased have had the same name. Names are not unique. But just a moment, when the hospital took your footprint and put it on record, *as happens with a fingerprint*, at that moment they recorded uniqueness. No one else living or deceased can duplicate your footprint. Your life is unique. Do not squander the uniqueness of your life by acting out the loser's role of conformity.

Shakespeare said, "All the world's a stage and all the men and women merely players." He is right. It is now your turn on the stage of life.

What role do you see for yourself? Will you have the leading role? Someone will be the star. Why not you? I can make this prediction with absolute certainty. Those who stand in the ranks of the conforming are destined to supporting roles, never the starring role.

Only the nonconformists can break out of the pack and take their places in the starring roles.

If you remember nothing else remember this; success, prosperity, peace of mind and financial security, all these attributes exist without prejudice. These attributes do not care about your past failure or about your age, sex, education or ethnicity.

Success comes to those who have the courage to leave the supposed security of the masses and strike out on their own no longer conforming to accepted practices. You must be ready.

The pseudo proverb *opportunity knocks but once* is totally false. Opportunity exists with *every new dawn*. There are literally millions of opportunities.

Those who conform to accepted practices are not prepared for opportunity so they end up thinking that it appears only once and they were out to lunch. Yet they miss multitudes of opportunities because they are not prepared.

Here are a number of proverbs that promote self-reliance. Incorporate these success principles into your life and life will yield to your desires; success will be assured.

The world does not owe you a living; it was here first.

*Do not mind what others
think; mind what you think.*

*Do not see things as they are;
see them as you want them to be.*

To think is to create.

There you have them, the four success axioms that guide a *self-reliant* person. It is your turn now to step forward and possess them, to be an example of the greatest lifestyle, the *self-reliant* life. Follow these proven concepts and success is in your future. You will be known as a person who lives the Richer Life.

*Love and Success Fit In The
Same Glove; They Are Inseparable.*

Rick C. Ernst

CHAPTER FIVE

THE SECRET WORD OF SUCCESS

There is one word more dynamic than any other having to do with success. When you understand this word intellectually and have released its energy emotionally, it will hasten the completion of your success journey more than any other word I know.

This word has broken down barriers of hostility, repaired wounded hearts and even given new life and meaning to people who were down and out.

This secret word makes the world go around. More has been written about this word than about any other word in the history of language. This word, above all words, will ensure your success.

This secret powerful success word is *love.* That's right, L-O-V-E, *love.* I describe *love* as the secret word of success not because you are unfamiliar with the word but because if you are like most people, you have little or no idea of the relevance of the word *love* as it relates to success.

Love and success fit in the same glove; they are inseparable.

I am about to reveal it to you one of the great success secrets of life. Years ago when I was first beginning to incorporate the success concept of the word love into my live events, many program directors, meeting planners and executives were taken aback and even embarrassed by my use of the word *love*.

Others forthrightly told me, "Do not use this word in your seminars." "Don't you know it's a dog-eat-dog world?" "Talk to us about power," they exclaimed. "Do not talk about love." Well, I have an insight for these people: *love is power*. And in this chapter you are going to discover why.

To fall in love with another person is a very natural thing. People do it every day. What you might not know is that to fall in love with success is also a natural thing to do. It is the healthy side of self-love.

I am sure you have known firsthand or have at least read about the dynamic changes that happen to people who fall in love with another person. Well, when you fall in love with success, dramatic changes also take place in your life.

I want you to consider three steps I will give you in this chapter as a guideline to falling in love with success. Each of these three steps are prioritized. You must take the First Step, before you can go on to Step Two and finally to Step Three. There are no shortcuts in this concept but there is finally full and lasting success.

STEP NUMBER ONE:
You Must Fall In Love With Yourself.

Love and respect for yourself is one of the biggest keys to a healthy self-image. You see, if you are your own worst enemy, if you are constantly running yourself down, sending messages to your subconscious that you are a failure, a nobody, a misfit, then you are headed straight toward a negative self-image and big, big problems.

There is no denying the enormous stress and pressure in today's world. Yet you are designed for success, designed to achieve, designed to overcome. Many people who live lives of success can testify that they began to achieve their success at the same moment they learned to truly love themselves and began to treat themselves as a person of great worth and potential. That is exactly what you need to do. I heard a wise man once say:

Once you've learned to love, you've learned to live.

What a wonderful insight is in this statement. When you feel good about yourself, about your future, then life takes on a different dimension. You see things in a different light. You see life as an opportunity. You are ready to carve out your place in life, ready to truly succeed. As Robert Browning said:

"Take away love and our earth is a tomb."

Browning is right. Without love there is only death. Our world owes to the force of love everything that is good and worthwhile about life. If at this moment you feel yourself bereft of love, it is not a mental or physical disorder—it is an educational problem.

Once you know how to love yourself, a new and more beautiful you will surge forth. So the first major hurdle is to fall in love with self.

Here are three ideas that will help you in your quest to develop a healthy self-love.

The first idea:

Stand in front of a mirror. Take a good look at yourself.

It may seem elementary but often a change as simple as different clothing or the manner in which you groom yourself will create a totally new feeling about yourself. Years ago the Gillette razor corporation ran an advertising jingle that suggested "When you look sharp, you'll feel sharp and you'll be sharp." That is sound advice.

While I do not believe that clothes make the man, I do believe that the clothes you wear often reveal the emotional and mental state of your mind and life. So spruce yourself up. You deserve it. You will like the new you.

The second idea to develop a healthy self-love:

Protect yourself from negative influences.
Put positive people in your life.

Much has been written about negativity and much will continue to be written. The bottom line is, as I said before:

You cannot afford the luxury
of negative friends or associates.

There is nothing in life as dangerous as negativity. No one who was negative about themselves and their opportunities in life has ever achieved success. You must learn to cast negativity aside and concentrate on the positive. Years ago, there was a hit song that said it best: *"You've got to accentuate the positive, eliminate the negative."* That is healthy self-love.

The object is to massage your mind with every type of positive reinforcement possible. Good, positive friends; positive-thinking books; self-improvement videos; personal growth events —all are important for your positive well-being.

However, nothing will ever serve you better than one, learning how to set positive specific goals for your life and two, placing yourself among positive, success-driven friends and associates. Loving yourself is not an oversimplification.

You will remain blinded to life's opportunities until you see yourself as worthy of success. So be sure your goals are clearly defined, surround yourself with positive friends and acquaintances, fill your mind with positive mental attitudes and drive the negative out of your life.

The third idea to develop a healthy self-love:

Develop a list of people
to whom you are important.

Think about it: you have parents, grandparents, cousins, aunts, uncles, a wife, a husband, children, grandchildren, peers, friends and coworkers. The list is endless. Most of these people will find you to be an important person, as will those in churches, social clubs and other organizations you support with your time, talent and money. Do you get the point? You are an important person. Life is better and made happier for many people because you are you and a part of their lives.

Over the years, lecturing and speaking in live events, I have witnessed scores of people who, when beginning to make a list of people to whom they are important, suddenly break out in tears. They simply did not realize how valuable they were to others. In this moment, they come to a dramatic new place in life. They realize for the first time that they are worthy, valuable and needed. What happens to them can happen to you. I know this:

Every person has value.
Every person has great worth.

That includes you, so before you read on, take a moment right now and commit to make a concentrated effort to discover the new you. Plan changes in attire or overall grooming to reflect the new you.

Eliminate from your life all forms of negativity and keep a list of people to whom you are valuable; add to it as you discover your greater value. The object is to take charge. Be the person you were designed to be, fully and dynamically successful.

STEP NUMBER TWO:
You Must Accept Each Member Of The Human Family Right Where You Find Them.

The diversity we find in America often troubles many people. Some think that America would be better served if we cleaned house ethnically, educationally and spiritually. However, people who know how to love, see the value of every person, no matter their nationality, age, education, religion or gender.

A person who knows how to love reaches out and embraces all mankind. A theme that pervades this book and almost every live event I have conducted concludes with this idea about success:

> ### *You are rewarded in life in direct proportion to the service you render.*

When your service to others includes treating everyone as if they are the most important person you know, success is your reward. In addition, to your personal success, by valuing others, you lift their spirits as well.

Karl Menninger said it best:

> ### *"Love cures people, both the ones who give it and the ones who receive it."*

Yes, love is a healing agent that heals all parties. Love does not recognize color, age or gender. It honors all men and women of all cultures. David Wilkerson makes a valid point when he says:

> ### *"Love is not only something you feel. It's something you do."*

That is the key. We do not even have to like everything about a person in order to love that person. Love is first and foremost a verb. Love is active, always seeking to do something meaningful. Love never says, "Well, if you do this or that I'll love you." Love loves on every occasion. Love never withholds its blessing.

The great thing about love, it is a wonderful gift to give to others, even those who oppose you. Love has a way of bringing out the best in you. Love challenges your motivation. Love demands that you be sincere, honest and self-sacrificing. Love develops character.

The greatest explanation of what love is and does has been captured for all time by a first-century AD disciple of Jesus Christ. His name was Paul. He explains the purpose, value and dynamics of love.

> *If I speak in the language of men and of angels but have not love, I am only a resounding gong or a clanging symbol.*
>
> *If I have the gift of prophecy and can understand all mysteries and all knowledge and if I have the faith that can move mountains but have not love, I am nothing.*
>
> *If I give all I possess to the poor and surrender my body to the flames but have not love, I gain nothing.*

Paul goes on to say:

> *Love is patient; love is kind. It does not envy, it does not boast, it is not proud. It is not rude, it is not self-seeking, it is not easily angered, it keeps no record of wrongs.*
>
> *Love does not delight in evil but rejoices with truth. Love always protects, always trusts, always hopes, always perseveres. Love never fails.*

One thing is for sure: when your motivation is derived from the pure fountain of love, your life will experience levels of excellence not possible otherwise. Let us examine sixteen of the adjectives Paul used to describe the value of love. You will quickly recognize that a man or woman who is ruled by love is destined for success.

First ***Love is patient***.

All of us admire the person who calmly waits out the storms of life, whose spirit of confidence never waivers.

Two: *Love is kind*.

Is there anything more valuable than to be treated kindly? Kindness is a soothing balm to the emotions.

Three: *Love does not envy*.

On the contrary, love rejoices when others have achieved greater happiness or position in life. Love is the first to say, "I am truly happy for you."

Four: *Love does not boast*.

Love has a quietness about it. Love lifts others up and plays self down. Love has a certain humility.

Five: *Love is not proud*.

This is undeniable. Love and pride cannot live in the same heart. Pride begets a certain failure in life; love lifts a person up to success.

Six: *Love is not rude*.

A rude person has victimized us all and it is not fun. Love, on the other hand, goes out of its way to be warm, friendly and understanding. Love seeks a warm-hearted settlement of differences. Love never demands its rights.

Seven: *Love is not self-seeking*.

On the contrary, love seeks the best for the other person. Love gives place to others, whether it is something as simple as opening a door or something more profound. Love seeks ways to promote others.

Eight: *Love does not delight in evil*.

In fact, love deplores evil. Love shuns evil but never the person. Love will embrace an evil person yet never the evil actions of their life. Love is sensitive and suffers when evil reigns within another's life.

Nine: *Love rejoices in the truth*.

Love and truth—where you find one, you find the other.

Love delights in the promotion of truth. Love will speak the truth even though the truth may convict a person of some shortcoming. Love speaks the truth not to hurt but to challenge a person to greater excellence.

Ten: *Love is not easily angered*.

This is my personal favorite. Love helps one to hold their temper, to remain calm and collected.

Eleven: *Love keeps no record of wrongs*.

Love is the author of a forgiving spirit. Love keeps no records or thinks in terms of "You'll get yours, just wait and see." Love knows that mercy is greater than judgment.

Twelve: *Love always protects*.

Love comes to the aid of those who are under threat or slander. Love steps in and serves as a protector.

Thirteen: *Love always trusts*.

Love always gives to others, each time and all the time, the benefit of the doubt. When it is unclear as to the truth of the matter, love always trusts.

Fourteen: *Love always hopes*.

No matter how dreary the outlook, how devastating the moment, love always looks forward in hope.

Fifteen: *Love always perseveres*.

Love stands firm. Love does not turn away when times get tough. Love stands its ground.

Sixteen: *Love never fails*.

It is just that simple. Love will, in time, always find a way to succeed. Love is the divine ingredient, the one healing, problem-solving agent of success.

People often exclaim, "I want to love others but my efforts, for the most part, are rejected. I'm not accepted. They will not let me in." Here is a great source of advice from Edwin Markham:

> *"He drew a circle that shut me out*
> *But love and I had the wit to win;*
> *we drew a circle that took him in."*

There is nothing like love. Though it may take time and you will have moments when it may seem as if nothing is changing around you, never fear. Love will work its miracle. Love is not an explosive force that knocks down barriers. Love is a gentle wave that seeks the heart of your fellow man. Its silent force, in time, captivates all who are recipients.

The secret to love's effectiveness is in direct proportion to its purity. For sure, love can be tainted. It can have all of the right signs yet be a love that does not complete its hoped-for goal. The Greeks of ancient days knew that love could be fractured and, as such, impure. Love, according to the Greeks, could be described as a high or low form. For instance, love could be classified as *Eros*. This is a Greek word from which is derived the modern word "erotic."

Eros love is a selfish form of love. It is given only when it knows there is a personal gain. Eros love is always pointed toward the self. It offers only what will be quickly returned to the benefit of the giver.

Another of the love forms of Grecian thought is *Phileo*. This is a form of love you will want to master. It is a love that will re-direct your energy, causing you to reach out to others, to help, assist and involve yourself for the benefits of others. The city of brotherly love, Philadelphia, comes from the word phileo. This is a great love, a love that moves mountains, a love that breaks through and embraces life's challenges and opportunities.

The third form of love identified by the ancient Greeks is *Agape*. This was, in the Grecian mind, the highest form of love one could offer to the benefit of others. I am quite sure the greatest example of Agape love is the life and work of Jesus Christ. He loved in spite of the rejection of his fellow man, the pain inflicted on him in physical abuse and the sacrifice he willingly made for others.

Agape love is pure love. Agape love seeks the best for others though its giver may not see any personal benefit for having so loved. This love is so special it never keeps score or records.

Agape love is just interested in loving. If the love you offer is not appreciated, so what? It was still right for you to love. It is always right to love. Yes, Paul was right. *Love never fails.*

> **Love is the first to say,**
> **"I'm sorry"**
> **and the first to express**
> **"I forgive."**

You see, love does not ever think about getting even or having to have its way or insisting on its personal rights. Love delights when others achieve. Love is the first to applaud another's good fortune.

Love is never selfish. Love causes you to arise early or stay up late for a good cause. Love seeks out the unloving, lifts up the downtrodden.

Ralph Trine hit the right key when he suggested, "Love is everything. It is the key to life and love's influences are those that move the world." The title of this chapter is *The Secret Word of Success.*"

Now you have it. "*Love*" is that special secret success word. Trine is right; *love is everything.* Its influence creates one success wave after another and the influence of love touches every fiber of life.

The object is to reach out in love to everyone you meet. The world responds to love. The love you give will find its way back to you in a multiplied harvest. You can count on it. Love never fails.

STEP NUMBER THREE:
You Must Fall In Love With Your Opportunities.

This is the third and final step in exploring the value and dynamics of love. When you think about life's opportunities, it is obvious that in the race to success and happiness we do not all start at the same gate. Some people in life are privileged; others suffer various disadvantages. Yet in spite of that, life has a way of providing opportunities to those who seek them.

When we do our best with each opportunity that comes our way, we open up greater and greater horizons for achievement and success.

The first thing that needs be recognized about life's opportunities is that *all work is sacred* and it is right to love your work even if it is not the job you want for the rest of your life. When you begin to stretch yourself in your work, to seize an opportunity, you are living on the sacred edge. You are living according to your design.

When you add love to work, you are totally on track for success and happiness. I can imagine someone who is reading now saying, "You don't realize the kind of work I have to do. It isn't fun. It isn't fair. It doesn't pay well." On and on and on they may go. Well, if you are that person, my response is, I may not understand the condition under which you work; but I do know this:

Love calls on you to blossom where you are planted.

Love will find a way when you are committed to success. However, you must learn to blossom where you are planted. Do your work like no one before you has done it. Do it better. Do it faster. Do it with enthusiasm. Do it with love.

Love your employer, love your supervisor and love those around you no matter what. Love your present opportunity and you will develop a frame of mind that allows you to spot other greater opportunities. Yes, embrace in love your present opportunity.

Have the desire to improve, the desire to please. Go the second mile. Be the best you can be. Let love become the prevailing force of your life. Remember:

> **Love opens doors.**
> **Love solves problems.**
> **Love pulls back the curtain of wisdom.**
> **Love is at the top of the list of success emotions.**

When Jesus was asked, "What is the greatest responsibility of man?" He answered. "To Love the Lord your God with all your heart and with all your soul and with all your strength and with all your mind and, Love your neighbor as yourself."

Love works when nothing else will. Start seeing yourself sharing love in all circumstances. Do this and one thing is for sure: you will have your priorities straight. You will never again be unsure how to act. No matter what others around you are doing, continue to love, treating your neighbor exactly in the same manner you would wish to be treated if the roles were reversed. This, then, is the secret word of success. *LOVE.*

To love life, its opportunities, its challenges, are the surest, fastest way to success.

Love will lift you to success

I am truly excited for you now that I know you have a greater under-standing of this powerful secret word. To the extent that you love, you are really alive.

Go quickly now. Throw yourself into the lake of life. Love will lift you over the highest wave and you will finally arrive on sunny shores, all of your dreams successfully achieved. All this is yours. Now! Today! Reach out and possess it! Start right now to love your way to success!

*Enthusiasm Is Not
Something You Get;
Enthusiasm Is Something
You Release From Within You.*

Rick C. Ernst

CHAPTER SIX

THE MAGIC QUALITIES OF ENTHUSIASM

I n a survey of two thousand businessmen, 85 percent said that greater enthusiasm was a huge need in their lives. If that thought has ever crossed your mind, then this chapter will be very valuable to you.

There is a totally invalid perception of *enthusiasm*, it is one you need to know about and knowing about it can change your life dramatically. I am amazed that this invalid perception has had such a long life but it has, so I want to settle things once and for all.

The misperception is that enthusiasm is something you must go forth to find. In the vernacular, we would say, "You need to get enthusiasm." Nothing is further from the truth.

> *Enthusiasm is not something you get;*
> *enthusiasm is something*
> *you release from within you.*

Here is one of the great insights about enthusiasm. This magnificent quality of life is given to human beings in equal amounts. The object is to release enthusiasm into your life. You presently have all the enthusiasm you will ever need. You are equal to all others in this marvelous quality.

In this chapter, I will share with you five great values of enthusiasm as well as seven dynamic ideas about how to release the enthusiasm that is already present in your life.

Here are the five great values of being an enthusiastic person.

THE FIRST GREAT VALUE OF ENTHUSIASM:
Enthusiasm Is A Universal Language.

One thing is for sure, it is never difficult to spot an excited person. Their speech and their mannerisms are always obvious. Even if people speak a language you do not understand, you can easily determine those who are enthusiastically going about their lives.

Enthusiasm is the same in any language. That is why enthusiasm is a universal language.

THE SECOND GREAT VALUE OF ENTHUSIASM:
Enthusiasm Serves As A Human Magnet.

Try this exercise the next time you are in a large group of people, perhaps a business meeting, party or church function. You will notice that people automatically divide themselves into small groups during the breaks in the meeting. Some know each other; some do not.

What is very clear is that in each of these groups, some people have a dominating influence on the others. Most often, it is the person exhibits the most enthusiasm.

This enthusiasm serves as a magnet and attracts others just as a moth is attracted to a flame. Yes, enthusiasm is a human magnet.

THE THIRD GREAT VALUE OF ENTHUSIASM:
Enthusiasm Is A Trigger
To People's Emotion.

The simplest way to express it is:

Enthusiasm breeds enthusiasm.

One excited person can stir up thousands. Human beings are emotional creatures and an enthusiastic person can tap into the emotions of others.

THE FOURTH GREAT VALUE OF ENTHUSIASM:
Enthusiasm Contains The Power To Drive Out Negative Thoughts And Negative Emotions.

As light dispels darkness, so enthusiasm accents the positive aspects of your life, helping you to limit or eliminate altogether the negative things that vie for your attention. Ira North said:

"Enthusiasm is as powerful as dynamite, contagious as measles and twice as catching."

He is right; enthusiasm is all this and more, a powerful, positive, potent ingredient that will enrich your life and give you a decided edge in the race to success. Yes, enthusiasm contains power.

THE FIFTH GREAT VALUE OF ENTHUSIASM:
Enthusiasm Is A Prime Method Of Persuasion Without Pressure.

Human beings for the most part are very predictable people. Many, for instance, will buy your product, your message, your dream if you share it with them in an enthusiastic manner. The rule is:

People buy more by emotion than by logic.

That is why an enthusiastic presentation will get results and your customer will not feel pressure. With enthusiasm you are operating in the most professional selling manner possible. You are a great persuader, not a person who deals in pressure tactics.

It is easy to understand the tremendous value of living life enthu-siastically. It changes you and soon those around you will begin to change. In the rest of this chapter, I will reveal seven dynamic ideas that you can use to release enthusiasm in your life.

Trust me on this: enthusiasm is already inside you. What you now need to do is find a way to release it into your life. I know the secrets to make this happen and I am now going to share them with you.

There are five life-changing ideas for becoming an enthusiastic person. Here is the first idea to release the enthusiasm that is already inside you:

Make sure your life is focused.

The single greatest reason most—and I emphasize the word *most*—people's lives are not going anywhere is that they are not focused; they have no vision. The great visionary of the ancient world, King Solomon, wrote:

"Where there is no vision, the people perish."

That is so true. The life that is excited, enthusiastic, is a life that has a vision, a focus and stays focused no matter what others are doing or not doing. You can always count on this fact:

Nothing great was ever achieved without enthusiasm.

The very fact that you focus on some great undertaking or you get a vision of some major idea will begin to release enthusiasm into your life if you hold onto it.

As if it were magic, this enthusiasm will become your ally; helping you stay focused and stay positive to keep on keeping on until you develop a plan that will ensure your success.

Here is how enthusiasm works regarding your focus, your vision. Enthusiasm is a telescope that yanks the misty, distant future into the radiant, tangible present. First there is the focus, the vision.

Then automatically comes the enthusiasm, an added ingredient for your success. It is like adding very fine oil to an engine. Its value is unending. Enthusiasm never wears out. As long as you keep the vision, you keep the enthusiasm. So keep the focus. How? Hold onto the vision for your life.

The second idea to release the enthusiasm that is locked inside you:

Reduce your focus, your vision to a specific goal and a written plan.

The easiest way to understand this idea is: if your focus does not become a specific goal along with a written plan, then your focus, your vision, is only a wish. You need to move beyond the wish stage, even beyond the want stage. You have to get to the must stage; then and only then, will enthusiasm rush into your life.

In Chapter Two I gave you an in-depth approach for how to establish specific goals and how to prepare yourself, developing a plan of action for your goal, your focus and your vision. The more you prepare yourself, the more you open up the resource of enthusiasm, which will then flow into your life and help you move forward to the completion of your goals.

Once again, I urge you to take time to prepare yourself for success by following the admonition of Chapter Two. Very carefully reduce your vision, your focus, to a clear, specific, written goal. Then begin to work on your plan of action.

While you are working on your plan, your life will become more and more exciting as enthusiasm is released to help you too finally and fully obtain the success you envision. Remember:

Your mind completes the picture you put into it and writing crystallizes thought.

The value of preparing yourself and reducing your focus to a specific goal and of developing a written plan is captured in an idea from Louis Pasteur. He said, *"Chance favors the prepared mind."*

Now to the third idea to release the enthusiasm that is locked up inside you is:

Above all else, be sure your goal, your plan of action, is one you can truly believe in.

The value of the third idea is that the emotional force of believing in your goal, having faith in yourself, will join with your enthusiasm and give you a great emotional edge. You will notice a new you beginning to emerge, as will others who are close to you.

People who believe in their goals, who are actively and enthusiastically engaged in creating success, are a force that cannot be stopped.

The bottom line:

When your goals are clearly set, with a strong belief, a dynamic faith, plus enthusiasm, your life will be headed straight toward success.

Here are two axioms from Jesus Christ:

One: *"If you can believe, all things are possible."*

Two: *"According to your faith, so be it unto you."*

The reason faith has such power in personal achievement is because it links itself in the emotional side of your life with enthusiasm. These two emotions, faith and enthusiasm, working hand in hand, create in your life a new dimension, a new positive and aggressive force— in fact, a new you.

The fourth idea to release the enthusiasm that is already inside you:

Visualize yourself succeeding.

Two major concepts are connected to this idea. When you master these two concepts, the natural enthusiasm that you have in your life will become the daily avenue to be used in your success journey.

The first concept:

Practice visualizations.

Henry Kaiser made a profound statement when he said:

"What a man can imagine or conceive in his mind, he can accomplish."

If this is true—and there are thousands of examples to support it, then you need to begin to practice visualization. Practice seeing all your goals coming true. The dominating thoughts of your mind will, in time, become your life. I have said it before but it bears repeating, because it is so significant:

Your mind completes the picture you put into it, and to think is to create.

A very ancient philosopher named Seneca added to this point when he said, *"Imagination begets the fact."* That is simple but it is also very powerful.

Do you want to give birth to a successful life? Well, begin now to visualize that life. Combine that visualization with specific goals and a written plan of action. Success will follow. When I suggest that you practice visualization, I mean that each day you set before yourself the dreams and goals of your life.

Find yourself a private place and private time, settle back, clear your mind and see yourself achieving each and every goal. It may not be easy to find this private place and time but it must be done. There are no shortcuts to success. It is not always easy but believe me; this visualization activity will pay rich dividends.

The second concept, in addition to practicing visualization, is:

Keep a success journal.

In this journal, this notebook, if you will, you list on a daily basis every positive thing that is going on in your life. Every time a goal is achieved, put it in your journal. Every time you hear a positive axiom, write it down.

Fill your journal with wonderful things that happen to you. Guess what? You will become more and more excited as you see yourself making progress on your journey toward complete success.

One idea behind this concept is that people are prone to live in the past. It seems to be the nature of the human species. If you are one of the majority who often lives in the past, your journal will be invaluable because your past, which your journal displays, is all positive; it is all good. That is the value of keeping a daily journal of your climb up the ladder of success. Keep visualizing yourself on Success Avenue and remain positive no matter how others act.

If you refuse to accept anything but the best, you will very often get it.

If your eyes are uplifted, if your desire is to live the excellent life, if you are determined to go to the top, to experience every level of success, including financial security, peace of mind and the highest levels of the good life, that is where you will end up. As Emerson said:

"The world makes way for the man who knows where he's going."

You can be that person. I have done it. Others before me have done it. And you can, too. Again I say, *to think is to create.*

The fifth idea to release the enthusiasm that is locked within you:

Avoid procrastination.

Whether you are new at the success game or an old pro, one thing that all can agree is there is a tendency to put off doing things you know need to be done. It seems even natural to put off activities, even to rationalize that we need to study the situation a bit more.

Procrastination is a disease of the mind and can create far more trouble than you might suspect. Procrastination, most of all, destroys the enthusiasm you have been building in your life. Knowing you are putting off important success activities sends a negative message to your heart and soon will start you on a downward spiral. The great humorist Will Rogers made a statement that truly applies to this point:

"Even if you're on the right track,
you'll get run over if you just sit there."

Nothing is more common than a person who, when beginning to achieve success, becomes self-centered, spending too much time thinking about their great achievements and not enough time moving on to the higher levels of success. These are moments when procrastination can sidetrack you and in some cases, send your success program into a tailspin. Being productive, step by step, over time will lead to success.

Successful people are not looking for a hill to climb so that they can then just sit down to review the success they have achieved. No, Successful people climb one hill in order to better see the next mountain to conquer.

Teddy Roosevelt, who was driven to be a man of excellence, a man of success, has a bit of advice that fits here. He said:

"Do what you can, with
what you have, where you are."

Now that is good advice. Each day the man who will achieve success will do what he can. In other words, he will get into action. He will start where he is with whatever tools are available. Procrastination is thereby eliminated.

There you have it: five dynamic ways to release enthusiasm into your life. If you are like most people, you have stood and watched high-energy, success-minded people move forth in their lives and you have wondered, "What is it these people have that I do not have?" The answer is "*nothing*." At this very moment, you have what you need to start your journey toward success.

I challenge you to become focused. Be visionary. Develop a plan of action. Reduce your goals to writing. Focus on only those concepts you can believe in. Visualize yourself a success. Affirm your success. Avoid negative people. And above all, avoid procrastination.

Even so, in doing all this there will be days on your journey toward success when you will not feel very excited. You will wonder about yourself. You may even say to yourself, "Rick Ernst can do it; maybe others can be successful but I don't feel I can." I have been there myself.

On those days, remember this: *do not* live your life based on how you *feel*; live your life based on what you *know*. And what you *know* is that enthusiasm is released into your life in direct proportion to the vision for success you hold in your heart. *So keep your vision before you!*

CHAPTER SEVEN

MASTERING THE TIME OF YOUR LIFE

O f all the concepts of success and prosperity, this subject is of supreme importance. The man or woman who does not consider the value of time and is not committed to make every effort to use each second in the most effective way, has failed to grasp the significance of what life is all about. Lost time is gone forever. Horace Mann had an exceptional understanding of the value of time. He wrote:

> *"Lost, yesterday, somewhere between*
> *sunrise and sunset, two golden hours,*
> *each set with sixty diamond minutes.*
> *No reward offered. They are gone forever."*

Does that sound like you? One thing is for sure: once time has passed, used wisely or not, the results are the same. That specific moment of time is gone forever.

This is not necessarily true with other aspects of life. For instance, if you lose wealth, it may very well be replaced through creative thinking and hard work. Misplaced research, hard-to-come-by knowledge, may be replaced through a dedicated commitment to restudy the subject. Lost health may be renewed with temperance, a closer watch of diet and exercise, better adherence to doctor's orders.

However, lost time is gone forever. You cannot make it up, cannot recapture it. It is thoroughly and completely gone.

As with every subject under the sun, the Bible offers sound advice on the subject of time. The Book of James shares this great thought: *"You do not know what will happen tomorrow. What is your life? You are a mist that appears for a little while and then vanishes."*

This does not mean that you are not important. You truly are! The point of this teaching is that your life is brief at best and each minute must be guarded and used as productively as possible.

Actually, the supply of time is a daily miracle, according to Arnold Bennett: *"You wake up in the morning and lo, your purse is magnificently filled with twenty-four hours of unmanufactured tissue of the universe of life."* It is all yours, the most precious of your possessions.

What you do with these twenty-four hours is always a very personal thing. The hours are yours. You can waste the moments that you have been given or you can invest them wisely. It is your choice. However, you must make a decision. Ben Franklin once wrote:

"Time is the stuff life is made of."

Whether your life is full or empty, time is provided to you freely. What you do with it spells failure or success. The dividing line between success and failure can often be expressed in just five words: *I did not have time.*

Every person on the face of the earth receives the same exact amount of time, that is, one day at a time. What we do with this time dictates our personal history. Time is ours but once; waste it and it is gone forever. Use it wisely and the fruit of your decision will prosper you. You will become the success of your dreams. It has been said:

Yesterday is a cancelled check; tomorrow is a promissory note; only today is legal tender, so invest it wisely.

Look at it this way: what you do today is extremely important. After all, you are exchanging a day of your life for it. Surely by now you understand the point. Time is a precious, valuable tool for building a life of success.

Wise use of the minutes, hours and days of your life will definitely pay rich dividends. The bottom line on mastering time is:

> ***Time is what we have;***
> ***wisdom is how we use it.***

In the remainder of this chapter, I will lead you through four valuable success laws concerning the wise use of time. All of these will be familiar to you, because I have introduced them in previous chapters. Yet if you are going to master the time of your life, you *must* utilize each of these four life-changing laws.

THE FIRST LAW:
You Must Establish Specific Goals For Each Area Of Your Life.

George Bernard Shaw once stated, "Life is no brief candle to me. It is a splendid torch that I want to make burn as brightly as possible before handing it on to future generations."

Far too many people are content with being a brief candle. They have few or no goals. As a result, they are pushed here and there by the winds of circumstance. Goal setters, however, are a different breed. They refuse to accept anything but the very best life has to offer. They realize they have it within themselves to be a splendid torch. They do not sit back and take what comes. They go after what they want.

So I challenge you to be *visionary.* Crystallize your goals. A man who would be a brief candle is a man of wishes. That is not you. Focus on your vision and dare to dream. The man who would be a splendid torch is a man of vision, goals and purpose. Above all, remember:

Living one hour of life totally
committed and dedicated, filled with
specific action, is worth years when your
spirit is submerged in apathy and self-doubt.

We pass through this life on earth but once. Make the most out of it.
Aim high. Be specific. I challenge you to dare to live out your dream.
Go for it. Make it happen. Others are doing it and you can, too.

It is a certain truth; men who become splendid torches are not much
different from other men, except in the intensity they bring to each
day's activities. It could accurately be said:

Great lives are ordinary lives intensified.

Brief candles often mistake motion for action. Splendid torches are
men whose lives are specifically ordered. They have a ready and sure
grasp of the big questions of life. Thus they are the masters of the
time of their lives and you can be too.

Here are four big questions to ask yourself about your goals. Your
answers will give you control over your actions and thereby allow
you to master your time. Ask yourself:

One: **What am I really setting forth to accomplish?**

Two: **What is the order of importance of the goals?**

Three: **What period of time have I set aside to accomplish
my goals?**

Four: **What are the best strategies for completing my goals?**

With the answers to these questions, you are now ready for success.

Thomas L. Forest said it best:

"A man's ambition should be high,
not scratched in the dirt
but carved in the sky."

That is the attitude of one who is to be a splendid torch. You see, when all is said and done, it is not failure that is a crime; rather, it is low aim. So look up to life with purpose, with anticipation, with the thought of winning. Remember: *to think is to create.*

THE SECOND LAW:
You Must Prioritize The Activities Of Each Day's Effort.

When I speak of prioritizing the activities of each day's effort, I am speaking of the art of in-depth planning. All time management, including prioritizing each day's activity, is in-depth planning. You plan your work and then work your plan. Once your goals are set, the next effort is to develop a plan, a specific plan that you can believe in, a plan that becomes your life, a plan that keeps you on track, driving you forth to the completion of your goals.

Therefore, each day without fail you review your plan, asking yourself, "*What is the best use of my time today?*" That is what I mean when I speak of prioritizing your activities. It is not enough to set specific goals or to develop a plan. You must constantly review your plan, applying new ideas, restructuring things that have been found to be inefficient, setting aside that portion of your plan that has proven unusable or unworkable.

In Judeo-Christian teaching, a man is encouraged to number his days, that he may apply his heart to wisdom. That is sound advice. To number our days is to consider the value of each day and to use it in the most efficient way.

In addition, the admonition is to apply our heart unto wisdom, that is, to think, to research, to find the wisest course for our life and to walk therein. That will include prioritizing each day's activity. Once you begin to live your life with a daily priority system, you will never want to go back to any other way of living and working.

Prioritizing your life's activities assumes you have set specific goals and have also developed a plan of action to reach them. That being a given, here is the most effective way to ensure that your life is prioritized, not just an occasional day here and there but every day of your life. This is how it works: at the end of each day before you leave your office or each evening before you retire, look over your goals and plans. Begin to review them and begin a list of the various activities that you need to accomplish tomorrow to stay on track to complete the goals you have established.

Once the activities have been listed, the object is to now give each of these activities a priority number. Whatever you consider the most important activity that you will engage in tomorrow, give it a number one priority rating. Whatever activity is next, list that activity as number two and then continue through your list giving each activity a priority number. Tomorrow when you arise, you are focused. You know exactly what activity to concentrate on; the object is to focus all your energy to completing your number one priority. I call this activity the *pre-day assessment*. Believe me; these few moments invested each day will pay you big dividends.

Here is what is so amazing about this pre-day assessment system. Even if it takes all day and 100 percent of your energy to accomplish the number one priority of the day, you still have had a great day. You accomplished the most important activity of your day. You are now one step closer to reaching your goal.

Begin using this proven system and I guarantee you will be successful. How can I state that so confidently? Easy, top achievers use this priority success system. When you have set specific goals and developed a personal plan of action, each day prioritizing your daily activities, you are definitely poised for success. One of the reasons so many people fail is that they lack a priority system. The result is that they often spend precious time engaged in activities of lesser importance. In addition, many times they will mistake motion for specific action.

Vince Lombardi stated:

"Winning is a habit."

When you develop the art of prioritizing each day's activities, it becomes a habit and that puts you on your way to the winner's circle.

It will happen. It has happened to me, it has happened to others and it will happen to you. Start now to develop the habit of prioritizing each day's activities.

THE THIRD LAW:
Each Day You Persevere Until Your Task Is Finished, Your Work Done.

Once you have decided the direction you have chosen for your life, then no matter what, you determine to persevere until you arrive at the very success you have set for yourself. It will always be true:

Successful people are those who hang on after others have let go.

Successful people persevere. They wisely invest their time concentrating their energies on the completion of their goals, rather than always running here and there seeking shortcuts to success.

I use the word *persevere* very carefully. It denotes challenge, setback, roadblocks, even failure. All of those things may be in your way. But remember this:

The greater glory is not in never falling down but in getting up when you fall.

That is the key. It is true; you cannot stop a person who will not quit. The successful person understands and knows that the reward far exceeds any pain one might be called on to endure while on the road to success. Therefore, time wisely invested through perseverance, though it may be painful, is one of the highest uses you can make of the time of your life.

Another thought linking perseverance with the wise use of time is:

Success is defined as finding happiness in something you finish, not in a thousand things started.

One thing that all successful people have in common is that they see each task through to its completion. That is, they finish things. In so doing, they press on. I have had to do this in my life. At times life has been hard, sometimes exceptionally hard but I chose to press on. So it is with you. I challenge you to press on.

- *Once you have decided what you want, press on.*

- *Once you have a plan of action, press on.*

- *Once you have prioritized each day's activities, press on.*

- *When negative people tell you it will not work, press on.*

- *When doubt tries to dissuade you, press on.*

- *Every day in every way, press on.*

- *Do not give up. Instead, look up to God for help, take the high road and always, always, press on.*

THE FOURTH LAW:
When The Day Is Over, Be Done With It.

Here are some great ideas you will want to ponder over and over again. This is the ultimate thinking on mastering the time of your life. Emerson provides you with four magnificent ideas that will ensure that you invest your time wisely.

One: *This day, today, is the best day of your life.*

Why? Today is the only day you have. No matter what is happening, it is still your best day. You have life and that means you have the opportunity to change things. You have precious moments to pursue your goals, to capture the American dream, to pursue life, liberty and excellence.

Two: **Own this day. Do not trade it for negative advice or self-doubt.**

I once visited an insurance executive who, on the back of his office door, had this quote: "I have met the enemy and he is me." How true that is. Each day is yours. It is given to you. Be a person of action not a person filled with self-doubt. Taking action is the surest prescription to fight self-doubt. Jesus challenged people to no longer doubt themselves. He offered this great insight. He said:

> **"If you can believe,**
> **all things are possible."**

What he was really saying was keep the faith and you will win the day. The day will be yours. Focus on the positive and the productive and you will own the day.

Three: **Do what you can; it will be enough.**

The person who does things will make many mistakes but he never makes the biggest mistake of all—doing nothing. If you honestly do what you can and by that I mean make a dedicated effort to do what you can, it will be enough. The time invested will be like putting good seeds in the ground. Soon you will reap a bountiful harvest. Regardless of what you might have heard, *work* is not a dirty four-letter word. Work is sacred. It is honorable. In fact, no rule of success is going to work if you do not. So remember do what you can; it will be enough.

I love this affirmation by Everett Hale:

> **"I am only one but I am one.**
> **I can't do everything but I can do something;**

And that I can do, I ought to do
And what I ought to do
by the grace of God I shall do."

This affirmation is so true. You are only one and being one, you cannot do everything. So just do what you can; it will be enough. Of course, when you take action, you do run the risk of failing but remember, as I said before, the greatest calamity is not to have failed but to have failed to try. I will say it one last time. *Do what you can; it will be enough.*

Four: **Keep a high spirit.**

Paul J. Myer, a man who built one of the leading personal development businesses in the world, has a great affirmation for people who have decided to take the high road. He said:

"Whatever you vividly imagine, ardently desire,
sincerely believe and enthusiastically act
upon must inevitably come to pass."

What a great thought idea. What a plan for life. What a vision for walking on higher ground, for keeping your spirit high.

Here are four great steps to keeping a high spirit.

One: **A high spirit is developed through imagination.**

The person you see in your imagination will always rule your world.

Remember,

To think is to create.

What you imagine about yourself will come to pass. Imagination is the life of your future.

Two: **A high spirit desires only the best.**

There is a great secret in desire. Here it is:

Desire creates the power.

Desire assists you to do things that you would have never tried before.

Three: *A high spirit lives by faith.*

There is nothing to help you conquer the challenges of life quite like a dynamic faith: faith in your creator, faith in yourself and faith in your goals.

Someone once said,

> *"If you can achieve your goals without God,*
> *your goals are not big enough."*

I believe that is true. I can tell you for sure that *big goals* take *big faith*. I will go a step further. To become the person you are capable of becoming requires faith, because faith sees beyond the challenge, the problem and the negative. It is amazing. First you have faith but soon faith has you. Then belief becomes real for you. You now see the unseen. You hope for that which without faith was hopeless. The exciting part is:

> *Faith acted upon*
> *produces more faith.*

Four: *A high spirit is full of enthusiasm.*

The Apostle Paul set forth this admonition: *"Be not slothful in business but fervent in spirit."* The word *fervent* is a code word for enthusiasm. Every great and commanding movement is the triumph of enthusiasm.

There they are the four dynamic success-coaching concepts for time management. As you put these ideas to work in your life, life as you know it will change. The world will not change but you will change. You will be different and this new and wonderful difference in your life will lead you to full and lasting success.

In putting this whole concept together, notice how the flow of these four ideas lifts you up and into another form of success-driven activity. When you establish specific goals for your life, you are lifted above the masses who have gathered around the first rung of the ladder of success.

Having your life prioritized, specifically on target, will give you an energy force, a killer instinct that will settle for nothing less than the best success life has to offer.

Through perseverance, you will find that at first if the door does not open, you check your approach and make another thrust, again and again. You stay at it, keeping the pressure on; finally you will win. At the end of the day, you accept this one day much like a prizefighter does. You traded blows with life. You win some rounds, you lose some but when a round is over, it is over. You are done with it. You refresh yourself and prepare for the next round, which is a totally new opportunity.

I can say to you in full confidence, make application of these truths and you will succeed. You will live to see your dreams come true and you will in fact, *master the time of your life*.

CHAPTER EIGHT

THE ART OF DEVELOPING FINANCIAL SUCCESS AND PERSONAL LIBERTY

O f all the questions I receive when speaking at live events, without a doubt the number one question most often asked in many different ways is: "What is the fastest way to become financially independent?" That is what this chapter is about, the art of developing financial success and personal liberty.

When we talk about becoming wealthy, a proper introduction for the coaching of the subject would be to consult with the source of all wealth. Are you aware that God has given us more verses of scripture devoted to finances and money and our proper use of them, than verses about heaven?

God knew that money was a practical matter that would require our attention on a daily basis. According to scripture money is a blessing of God, given so that we might be good stewards of a portion of the Lord's bountiful supply. In addition, God often uses money as a tool to test our trust and faithfulness.

There are three main principles in God's word regarding money and material wealth or as I call it in this chapter, financial success and personal liberty.

First, God is the source of all blessings and wealth. *All wealth comes from God.*

> *"You may say to yourself, my power and the strength of my hands have produced this wealth for me. But remember the Lord your God, for it is he who gives you the ability to produce wealth and so confirms his covenant, which he swore to your forefathers, as it is today."* Deuteronomy 8:17–18

Second, material possessions are *not* eternal. All possessions become outdated, break, decay or get used up. The proper way to see material possessions is as temporal and as tools to be used and enjoyed while we strive to accomplish our goals that God has helped us to set.

Third, the pursuit of money should never be our main focus. Sure, we all have bills to pay and we need money to properly function in society. It goes without saying that all dreams have to be funded.

Given this basic understanding of meeting our daily cash flow needs, our attitude should be to be of service, first to God and then to others. The secret to becoming a financial success is to, *find a need and fill it.* This thought points to being of service to others.

This may be a good time to remind you of my definition of the *Richer Life* which is found in the front of this book:

> **A consciousness of humility
> and service to others, in unison
> with the ongoing pursuit of obtaining and
> maintaining balanced and abundantly fulfilled
> relationships, possessions and esteem in every area of life.**

Now that we have put becoming a financial success in its proper light, in this chapter I will provide you with the wealth-building secrets that, in the twentieth and now the twenty-first century, have lifted millions of men and women out of poverty and debt into the *Richer Life*, into the world of financial success and personal liberty.

It is almost certain that achieving financial success will not be easy but it can be done. Others are doing it. So can you. The key to it all, the first and ultimate priority, is *you must have a plan*. I am going to help you here. I have a plan for you, a plan that never fails.

A specific insurance statistic speaks to the subject of wealth and financial success. You may have read it or heard about it. Let us look at it in the light of our quest for financial success. Of one hundred men with a dream of retiring from their labors with financial success, thirty-six died before they reached retirement age.

Second, of these one hundred men, five, having reached retirement, were still working. They simply were not yet financially secure enough to begin retirement.

Thirdly, fifty-four of the hundred men were no longer working but they were not financially successful, either. Others were providing for them, the state, relatives, charitable institutions, etcetera.

Please understand that I am not placing blame on or criticizing these fifty-four men. I'm simply relating the facts. Finally, out the hundred men who began their vocational life with a dream of becoming financially successful, retiring to the *Richer Life*, secure in their lifestyle, five were able to achieve this goal. Only five became fully financially secure. The question must be asked. *"What did these five men discover that brought them success?"* That is what this chapter is all about: discovering the ultimate secret truth of developing financial success and personal liberty.

As strange as it sounds, the most difficult task before me is not to lead you to an understanding of the secrets of financial success. I am confident I can do that. The task for me is to get you to believe you can become financially successful. That is always my biggest challenge. Difficult though it may be, I am committed to presenting the facts about financial success in such a way that you will just have to believe them. How does one move toward financial success? First, you need to be made aware of the talents and developed abilities you presently possess. I can hear someone saying "Me?" Yes, you.

There are six things I know about you, all of them very good things. I know you have everything you need to create financial success, yes, these great things are in your possession right now: six positive financial success-building abilities.

In the next few pages, I will coach you on how to harness these innate abilities and skills. That's the first step.

Second, the five priorities that regulate the secrets of financial success and yes, I am going to reveal these secrets to you, secrets that have provided financial success for millions of men and women.

To understand the six innate and developed talents that you possess, the best approach may be to look at your life in the same way you would define a business corporation. A corporation has certain assets, inventory and potentials for success and so do you.

Here are six assets I know you possess that can be used to lead you to financial success.

One: ***You possess the assets of know-how and experience.***

Whatever your age, if you are old enough to seriously consider this book, you have certain valuable abilities, talents, work experiences and know-how, which, when strengthened, enlarged and energetically utilized, will help lead to financial success.

Two: ***You have in your control a dimension of time.***

No one knows exactly how much time they will be given for work, for retirement or even for life. However, today you possess twenty-four hours of unblemished opportunity. Learning how to invest the time of your life wisely will help to ensure your financial success.

Three: ***You possess the highest form of energy and power for success the world has discovered –human energy.***

When it is all said and done, your success will be the sum total of small steps, one after another, day in, day out.

Four: *You possess a unique creative imagination.*

You have the ability to see what needs to be done and how to accomplish it. That is imagination. When you harness your imagination, crystallizing your thoughts into specific goals, you are on your way to financial success.

Five: *You possess the power of concentration.*

Concentration is a very special key to unlocking the door to financial success. By concentrating 100 percent on your life's priorities, your efficiency will soar; your dream of financial success will come true.

Remember:

To think is to create.

Six: *You posses the ability to make successful decisions.*

You have within you the power of choice. Yes, you can choose success.

Carl Fredrick said:

"The key to your universe
is that you can choose."

He is right. Proper choices in life create financial success. Now let us summarize your personal assets. When you put them all together, it is plain to see you are a very special person. You have know-how, experience, time, energy, a unique creative imagination, the power of concentration and decision-making ability. That is a dynamic list of assets. One thing is for sure: with these qualities in your life, you are poised for financial success. All you need now is a proven plan. I have that plan and soon it will be yours.

When I say I have the plan for your financial success, I do not mean to infer that it is my plan. This plan for financial success has been handed down through the ages. It is time-tested. It is comprised of the best financial ideas Western civilization has perfected.

The plan has five distinct areas that regulate the success a person will enjoy. When you utilize each of the five concepts, putting them in your life with enthusiasm and hope, you are on your way. Your dreams will come true; it is just a matter of time.

THE FIRST PRIORITY FOR FINANCIAL SUCCESS:
Accurately Determine Your Present Financial Condition.

Tragic to say, most people do not know where they stand financially. Some are so confused they will require professional help. Most likely, though, that will not be your problem. However, if it is, get help now. If you are like most people, your problem will be simply one of getting organized, finding out exactly where you are financially and developing a plan to move forward to where you want to be financially.

There are a vast number of books and computer software you can purchase to help you understand your true financial condition. Many can be purchased for less than fifty dollars. Though these financial aids are available, many people still refuse to confront their financial condition because of its bleak outlook. Do not make that mistake. You must get your financial condition out into the open once and for all, where you can finally set forth the ways and means for positive change leading to full and lasting financial success.

THE SECOND PRIORITY FOR FINANCIAL SUCCESS:
Determine To Eliminate Debt From Your Life.

In the past decades, the rage among many financial advisors was that you should constantly leverage your assets as deeply into new debt as you possibly could and inflation and quick depreciation schemes would bring a sure and financial leverage. However, it has been proven over time that whenever you go into debt, with or without the advice of a financial planner, you do so at your own peril.

In my own experience and through much research, I have discovered that some of the best advice and truly wise thoughts about debt are found in the Bible. Take note of what King Solomon said:

"The borrower is servant to the lender."

There is also this famous line from the Apostle Paul: *"Owe no man anything, except the continuing debt of love."* Believe me,

- *Debt Destroys!*

- *Debt Cripples!*

- *Debt Burdens!*

- *Debt Limits!*

If you are not now in debt, stay clear. If you are in debt, begin a plan to escape.

THE THIRD PRIORITY FOR FINANCIAL SUCCESS:
Develop A Saver's Attitude.

The people who will never feel the special satisfaction of discovering success for their life will surely be the people who fail to develop a saver's attitude.

Not too long ago in America, the financial philosophy about success changed. Americans were led to believe that you could borrow your way to success. The outcry was, "If you can qualify for a loan, do it, borrow all you can. Have your cake and eat it too." This is very different from past generations, when men, women and families achieved full and lasting success and often never borrowed the first penny. Today we are told those days and times are over. The world has changed. No, the world has not changed. Attitudes have changed. My hope is that I can present eight life-changing yet simple ideas that will convince you of the value of developing a saver's attitude, that you will be challenged by these ideas, that you will take them into your life, making them a part of your thinking process and that you will live them fully and completely.

The first idea:

Accept financial success as your birthright and commit now to always save out of your present abundance.

That idea leads me immediately to the second idea:

Part of all your earnings is yours to keep if you will.

These first two ideas go together. Whatever your present financial condition, you are potentially a winner, a success. No matter how small your present income, part of that income can and must be saved if you are going to become a financial success.

I do not care if all you can save is a dollar a week; start there. Soon you will discover ways to save even more. The rule is simple:

You must always be saving.

The third idea:

Do not wait for others to help you with saving. You can do it yourself.

I doubt that in this one book I can convince you that everything you need to achieve success in your life resides within you but that is the truth. However, that does not rule out the need to search for wise counsel, to read, to study, to ask questions of other successful people. You will want to do that but in all your searching, remember this:

You are designed for success.

It is true; you are a potential financial success. Start by becoming a saver now.

The fourth idea is once again from Emerson:

> ### "If you can't save money, the seeds of greatness are not in you."

It is obvious Emerson knew of the common temptation to spend unwisely, to attempt a shortcut to financial success, to mortgage yourself into success. Actually, saving money is a test: a test of your will, a test to determine whether you will be a full and lasting success or a spark that quickly dies in the wind. Relish the test.

Decide now that you are going to be one of the few that make it to the ranks of the successful. You are going to be a saver, which means, in time, a financial success.

The fifth idea:

> ### Being broke is temporary; being poor is a state of mind.

What you will discover on the road to financial success is that the reason most people never arrive at a level of success in which they find peace of mind, prosperity and financial liberty is because of this basic axiom: poverty is a state of mind.

Think about it. What have you lost when you have lost money?

If you have your health, time, energy, dreams and goals, you will soon be on top again. Being broke is simply one of the states of reality you might experience as you pursue success.

You will discover just how true this can be as we look at the sixth idea for developing a saver's attitude.

> ### If you fear going broke, you will never be rich.

The simple reason this is true is *that fear and faith cannot live in the same heart.* If fear rules, you are always going to settle for less than the very best. You will not have sufficient faith to be a daring success. Fear is a strong and toxic emotion. Fear creates all sorts of compromising attitudes. Fear holds many people in its grip.

You do not have to practice fear to be consumed by it. Fear seems to take on a life of its own, corrupting the future, making the present an unhappy existence. Faith, on the other hand, seems fragile. It must be supervised constantly, must be reinforced, promoted and held too tightly. All that is true but faith is the ingredient that produces the sunshine; fear brings forth the darkness. Faith produces creativity, the positive side of life; fear produces the negative, the doubt, the lie. As a great hymn suggests, faith is the victory.

The seventh idea:

> ***If you lose wealth, you have lost much.***
> ***If you lose friends, you have lost even more.***
> ***If you lose your self-esteem, you have lost everything.***

This is the very reason I repeatedly say: *Success is your birthright!*

It is a natural right of man. It cannot be given to you; it is already a part of you at birth and I might add you are the crowning glory of God's creation. You were destined for success. When you stand erect, when your head is not bowed, when all around you, others are quitting but you are unmoved, then success will shine upon you.

> ***If you have made up your mind you***
> ***will not be defeated, never will you be.***

Look at yourself in the mirror. Yes, you are male or female but you are more than that. You are unique, one of a kind. You are a new energy here on this planet. Take your place with the winners of life. It all begins inside of you. When you are ready, the world's ready. It is really that simple. So start being a saver. It will help lead you to financial success.

The eighth idea:

Blossom where you are planted.

One constant in history suggests that many people who miss success do so because they quit their present position too soon.

Here is the overall principle of this eighth idea. Ask yourself "Have I given my very best to this job opportunity? Have I done this job as well or better than anyone who has been assigned to it? How can I make this job more enjoyable? How can I make myself more valuable through this position?" That is to, blossom where you are planted. Give 150 percent, not just one day but every day. One of my favorite Bible verses fits here. It is Colossians 3:23–24:

> *"Whatever you do, work at it with all your heart, as working for the Lord, not for man, since you know that you will receive an inheritance from the Lord as a reward. It is the Lord Christ you are serving."*

It must also be said, that if the door of increased opportunity is not open to you in the job you now hold and if it is truly a dead-end job, you will know it, if you have given 150 percent effort to it. Then if greater opportunities are not forthcoming, cut your losses, break out and seek diligently the job of your dreams. Jesus said:

"Ask and you shall receive,
seek and you shall find,
knock and the door will open."

Therefore, exercise your faith.

- *Start asking!*

- *Start seeking!*

- *Start knocking!*

- *Start today!*

Then keep asking. Keep seeking. Keep knocking. You know what? The door you need will open!

> *God wants to show you how powerful he is.*
> *So humble yourself and ask Him to help you.*

Remember the proverb that God helps the humble but sets Himself apart from the proud.

THE FOURTH PRIORITY FOR FINANCIAL SUCCESS:
Set Specific Goals To Become Financially Successful.

One of the truly great benefits of being a goal setter is that you automatically focus your mind and energies on your future possibilities, not on your present problems.

It does not cost you one penny to take pen and paper in hand and to begin to dream your very own dream of financial success. Start your dream with a thorough understanding of your present financial status, a goal to meet your basic financial needs and a goal to eliminate your debt.

When those three things are accomplished, you are now ready to dream additional dreams, to set forth your financial goals. At this point you will be ready for swift and sure success.

If you have a family or if you own your own business or both, it is a good idea to include your family and key members of your business in your goal-setting activities. When there is unity of agreement on what the goals are, your combined energy level will increase dramatically. So set your goals. Dare to dream a big dream.

Here are the three steps to financial success:

One: *Have a complete understanding of where you are and where you want to be financially.*

Two: *In setting your goals, begin with goals that meet your present financial needs with an additional amount for debt reduction.*

Three: *Now add your personal financial dreams for the future. See yourself becoming an outstanding success.*

THE FIFTH PRIORITY FOR FINANCIAL SUCCESS:
Develop A Money Management Plan Of Action And Start To Work It Immediately.

When you first start to use a money management plan you may have to curtail certain activities, adopt new habits and maybe even a new lifestyle. You may have to cut up your credit cards or lay them aside for the time being. Whatever it takes, commit to it.

I challenge you to know the thrill of finally having the burden of debt out of your life. John Maxwell says:

> *"A budget is telling your money where to go, instead of wondering where it went."*

I coach people on how to become financially independent by setting aside a portion of their earnings to be used for various purposes. The following technique will teach you to be more specific with your money distribution for better money management and control.

This financial success concept will give you instant control over the flow of your money, which will lead to financial liberty. Let me encourage you to start using this money management system now. I said to start using it when? *Now!* It does not matter that you may only have a little money when you start to use this system. What does matter is that you start *now* to use this proven system. Even if all you have to start with is just fifty dollars, ten dollars or even only one dollar. When you start using this system the simple act of using, it will train your mind how to properly handle your money. To use the following money management system you will need to open *seven checking accounts* and *name each account* as per the instructions below.

It is wise to use a financial institution that does not charge a service charge for checking accounts. Open each account with the minimum amount of money required.

The below percentages for all seven checking accounts are *only* recommended percentages. You may have to change them to fit your own set of circumstances depending on your income.

If you have a low income, your household necessities percentages will be high. If you have a high income, your household necessities will be a lower percentage of your income and then you can put a higher percentage of your income into your other checking accounts.

As you use this money management system remember, *it is very important to always use all of your seven checking accounts.*

The seven money management checking accounts are:

1. GOA – *General Operating Account*

Into this checking account, you will deposit *100 percent* of your earnings. Then you will disburse the appropriate percentages to your other checking accounts listed below. You can easily do this by banking over the Internet. The rest of the accounts below are funded with after-tax dollars.

2. TEST – *Tithe, Offerings and Charitable Giving Account*

Deposit *10 percent* into this checking account. Regardless *of your income, 10 percent should be the minimum you put into this account.*

I named this account the *TEST* account because when dealing with this percentage of our income God challenges *us, gives us a test* to handle it in the proper way.

"Bring the whole tithe into the storehouse, that there may be food in my house. Test me in this," says the Lord Almighty, "and see if I will not throw open the floodgates of heaven and pour out so much blessing that you will not have room enough for it. I will prevent pests from devouring your crops and the vines in your fields will not cast their fruit," says the Lord Almighty. Malachi 3:10 -11

In addition to the tithe, we are encouraged to be givers. Acts 20:35 says: *It is more blessed to give than to receive.*

The word *blessed* here means to *cause to prosper.* Some people mistakenly think that tithing, offerings and charitable giving are all the same thing. The Hebrew word for *tithe* literally means *tenth* or *ten percent.* We *owe* God *10 percent* of our income, which is called the *tithe.* The tithe is to be given where you are spiritually fed.

Offerings are what we give above and beyond the tithe. Remember the tithe already belongs to God and we are just returning it to him. That means our giving really begins with our offerings and charitable contributions. Offerings are our financial seeds planted into the kingdom of God. Our charitable contribution is the money we give to help organizations and associations continue the work they are doing.

With this understanding, you may be wondering if our tithe is to be at least *10 percent.* Why do I say to only put 10 percent into this account, remember the percentages are to be used as a guideline. My coaching is to always return a minimum of *10 percent* to God first and then give in other ways. Proverbs 3:5, 6-9, 10 contains the wisdom for passing this lifelong financial test.

Trust in the Lord with all your heart and lean not on your own understanding; in all your ways acknowledge him and he will make your paths straight ... Honor the Lord with your wealth, with the first fruits of all your crops; then your barns will be filled to overflowing and your vats will brim over with new wine.

Your tithe *opens the door to God's blessing* and as he increases your income, you will be able to pay your household bills on *less than* 50 percent of your income.

Then you can increase the percentages you put into your other accounts. This will enable you to give even more tithes, offerings and charitable contributions.

3. HNA – *Household Necessity Account*

Deposit *50 percent* into this checking account. This account is used for paying your daily living expenses, such as:

HOUSING: First mortgage, second mortgage, repairs, maintenance and homeowner's association fee.

FOOD and UTILITIES: Food, electricity, water, gas, phone, trash, TV/cable and Internet service.

TRANSPORTATION: Car payments, gas, oil, repairs, tires and car insurance.

PERSONAL: clothing, toiletries, laundry, dry cleaning, disability insurance, health insurance, life insurance, childcare, etcetera.

OTHER: miscellaneous items.

4. CAE – *Coaching and Education*

Deposit *10 percent* into this checking account.

School is never out of the question for the true professional. You must continue to expand your horizons and education through reading positive books, listening to personal growth materials, coaching and attending life-changing events. All of these activities will keep you on the cutting edge.

5. PII – *Passive Income Investments*

Deposit *10 percent* into this checking account. Passive income is income received on a regular basis, with no or little effort required to maintain it.

During my live events I am often asked, "When is someone *financially rich?*" here is my definition:

> **You are financially rich when:**
> **When your passive income exceeds**
> **the expenses of your desired lifestyle,**
> **leaving you with money to save and invest.**
> **Working for money is now, an optional activity.**

Therefore, in order to become *financially rich* you will need to make investments and purchases and perhaps participate in entrepreneurial efforts, all of which will create for you *multiple passive-income streams*. It is very important you understand and agree to *only use the money in your PII account to create passive income*.

6. IFM – *Instant Fun Money*

Deposit *10 percent* into this checking account.

In this account, you reward yourself by setting aside 10 percent of your earned income for *instant fun money*. The money in this account will cover items like going to the movies or other forms of entertainment and fun. Perhaps you want to take a trip to a neighboring city and stay in a great resort for a few days or maybe enjoy a day at the spa. That is how this account is to be used. This money is best used for doing things you might not *normally* do.

The rule for the money in this account is you *must spend all of the money* in your *IFM* account *each month and* you can spend it any way you like, totally guilt-free. In short, this money is the money for the things that make you feel like you are living the *Richer Life*.

7. SFS – *Savings For Spending*

Deposit *10 percent* into this checking account.

In your SFS account, you save for items such as a car, boat, truck, furniture, household repairs and improvements or even an exciting family vacation. If you are saving for multiple items, you will open other SFS accounts, one for each item. Then split the 10 percent evenly among your SFS accounts. For example, 5 percent *half* of the 10 percent will go to the SFS boat account and 5 percent will go to the SFS new furniture account.

This is a proven money management and debt reduction system. If you have the courage to use it, I guarantee that in time you will be among the people achieving financial success and enjoying personal liberty. Here is one last thought on the subject of money management. Once again, it is from the pen of Ralph Waldo Emerson.

> ### *"If you want to be rich,*
> ### *make your wants few and find*
> ### *a way to supply those wants yourself."*

There are two great ideas in this advice from Emerson. First, he presents a way to look at success that few in this generation know anything about. Emerson is saying that riches consist in not pursuing every whim but in finding satisfaction in the few obvious basic needs that make life manageable. Secondly, where Emerson speaks of supplying your own needs, in today's global marketplace you have opportunity to do just that.

My favorite way to build wealth has always been investing in real estate. This has created more millionaires than any other sector, such as stocks and bonds, gas, oil or precious metals. *Seventy percent of all millionaires are made through investing in Real Estate*. Why is this? It is because investing in *Real Estate, if done right* has the potential to create big income at an amazingly rapid rate. In both good and bad times, one thing is for sure. *Real Estate* investing is the safest of all investments.

To begin receiving my *FREE* weekly *Real Estate Investing Tips*, go to www.MyRicherLife.com and enter your name and email address at the bottom of the menu on the left-hand side.

Now that you understand how to manage your money and have begun the process of setting goals to achieve financial success, you will want to consider very carefully the following question:

Why are the financial goals I have chosen important to me?

Not to preach but my experience convinces me that most people are running head-over-heels for things, all kinds of things, without really considering the cost or the true value these things will have in their life. For sure,

Success is sometimes based not on how many things you acquire, but on the things that, you do not have to have.

Most agree that prudent people are usually the most successful. That is because they think long and hard about their success, about their plan for lasting financial success. Their budget is often uncluttered with the latest happiness gimmick.

They lay out their plan in a conservative style, knowing: One, that debt is the enemy and two, that developing a money manager's attitude and spirit is the road less traveled but the one with the greatest promise.

Here are five steps to help you assemble your financial success plan of action:

1. *Focus your mind on the exact amount of money you want to earn each year.*

2. *Subtract what you now earn from the amount you want to earn and you have your target for increased income.*

3. *Begin an idea book wherein you will enter all ideas that might help you reach your income goal.*

Write down the ideas as you think of them, read about them or perhaps pick them up from a friend or while attending a seminar. However they come to you, store them in your idea notebook. Soon one or more of these ideas will grow in your mind and can help you to reach your income goals.

4. *Start now, right now to use the seven-checking account money management system.*

When developing your budget for this system, use your present income level, not what you hope to earn in the future.

5. *Live within your set income percentages for each of your seven checking accounts.*

In addition, continue working creatively to increase your income. As I have said before, be sure you are take advantage of every opportunity for personal growth by reading more books and always, that means each day; make a habit of listening to positive self-improvement materials. This rule is a simple one; when you are *still* you are *reading*, when you are *moving* you are *listening*.

For accelerated learning and growth, attend as many high-impact personal growth events as you can. These kinds of activities put you on track to build a life of financial success.

Using this proven plan of action is important but more important is your attitude toward your financial success. The truth is, when you are ready for financial success, you can have it. If your resolve is firm, your desire intent, your goals crystal-clear, you are on your way to financial success.

Once you have adapted the above money management system and chosen the right percentages of your income to use for each of the checking accounts, take the time to write down the specifics of your money management plan and keep a copy with you at all times.

Each morning and each evening read your financial plan of action to yourself. Modify and expand your plan as needed as your income and lifestyle change. Then once again, take the time to write down the specifics of your plan and then burn the new key elements of your money management system into your subconscious.

Become so familiar with your money management plan that you can recite it at a moment's notice. Then and only then can you say, "I am ready. Financial success is my destiny."

Now you have in your possession the same success concepts that all wealthy individuals know and use. Make application of these *Richer Life* financial success secrets and you will take your place as a *master of your money*, a person who knows, enjoys and lives with financial success.

Remember, it does not matter where you are right now, on the ladder of financial success. You now have the financial *Richer Life Secrets* to climbing up and up until you reach the top, where you will enjoy the exciting life of financial success and personal liberty.

It Is Not The Ability You Have
That Makes You Successful;

It Is How You See
And Use Your Ability
That Determines Your Success.

Rick C. Ernst

CHAPTER NINE

BUILDING A POWERFUL, HEALTHY SELF-IMAGE

S o much has been said and written on the subject of a good self-image that you would think everyone would have heard the last word on how to build and maintain a healthy self-image.

I learned a long time ago that just talking about a problem never solves it. You must identify the problem, find the answer and then *apply* the answer to the problem. This is doubly true of building a powerful, healthy self-image.

While hundreds of books about self-image psychology continue to pour forth on a regular basis, very little has been written that really answers the problem of how to combat a poor or low self-image and build a powerful, healthy, positive self-image. One thing is for sure. When it comes to a healthy self-image, you do not have to be sick, to get better.

What you think is what you get.

As far back in history as we find recorded events, men were then reminiscing on the subject of self-image. The Creator, as set forth in Judeo-Christian teaching, was said to have made man in his own image and able to experience free will. That is, man had the freedom to choose the path he would follow.

Based on this understanding, King Solomon set forth an enlightening foundational statement, a real key to understanding self and our image of self. This is a familiar statement.

"As a man thinks in his heart, so is he."

I challenge you to let this great truth sink deep into your heart and mind. What Solomon is saying is whatever you think about most will become the ultimate direction of your life. Though written 3,500 years ago, this remains a fundamental truth: "as a man thinks in his heart, so is he." Not until the early part of the twentieth century, did a person restate Solomon's great truth in such a way as to give us another great insight into ourselves. Dr. William James said:

"A person can change the direction of their life by changing the direction of their thinking."

King Solomon defined the problem when he said, as a man thinks so he becomes. Dr. James answered the problem when he said, if you are not happy with yourself, change the way you think and your life will take on a new direction.

This I know to be true:

Every waking moment, you are thinking about something.

That is just human nature. Here is the exciting part: you do have a choice as to what you are going to think about. That is right! You do have a choice. I can hear someone saying, "Rick, you don't know me. You don't know how messed up my life has become." Well, you are right; I may not know you personally but I do know this: you can think only one thought at a time. So you do have a choice.

You can decide what you are going to think about. Successful people, people with healthy, powerful self-images, are no different from you. They too can only think one thought at a time. Successful people choose to think the best about themselves. So can you. You do have a choice.

I will now coach you on how to make the proper choices. The main point to remember is that your thoughts, your choices of what you think about, give birth to ideas and your ideas have consequences. So if the result you want is a powerful, healthy self-image, then go back to the basics. Choose your thoughts carefully and the rest will take care of itself.

In this chapter, I will introduce to you four great success secrets for building a powerful, healthy self-image through wise choice of thoughts. As you take hold of and practice these four concepts, you will begin to change. It is not an overnight process but it will happen. It must. It is the nature of how things work.

THE FIRST GREAT SUCCESS SECRET:
Only Shallow Men Believe In Luck.

Ralph Waldo Emerson wrote these compelling words in the early 1800s. They remain true to this very day. There is no such thing as *luck*, yet people use the word all the time. Even successful people often say, "I've been lucky." That is never true. Things turn out the way they do for a reason. The law of reciprocity is at work every-where in the universe. For every cause there is an effect. All of humanity and all of nature are in submission to this truth.

Let me ask you a question; have you noticed people whose lives are not going anywhere often say things like "If I didn't have such bad luck, I would not have any luck at all?" That is a gross exagge-ration of reality. You have bad luck—or, I should say, have bad results—when your *thinking is stinking*. You have good luck or good results, when your *thinking is success-oriented*. That is the law. Again, whatever you think about most is what will happen to you.

Stop for a minute and consider your life to date. Let us say you are not the successful person you would like to be or maybe you are the only one in your family who is not already successful or maybe you are successful but not to the level of your dream.

So what is the first step to turning your life toward more success?

Consider this:

> **To start to turn your life toward more success,**
> **accept responsibility for where**
> **you are in the now of your life,**
> **but do not blame yourself.**

There is a huge difference between accepting responsibility and assigning blame. Why you are where you are, may involve hundreds of related matters and I can state for certain, that you are not to blame for all of them. So first, get blame out of the way.

Second, start now to take responsibility for your life, get up and dust yourself off, if need be. You are not an unlucky person. You are only a person who has mishandled some of the circumstances of your life. However, once you take charge of your thought process by accenting the positive, you will begin to move in a new and dynamic direction. Good luck? No! *Good results* will be the order of the day. That is a promise from me to you!

THE SECOND GREAT SUCCESS SECRET:
Always Demand Of Yourself
A Spirit Of Self-Help.

Samuel Smiles wrote:

> *"The spirit of self-help is the root*
> *of all genuine growth in the individual."*

Sometimes I wish this statement could become the law of the land. The concept is a law in the world of success ideas but I am thinking in terms of what local, state and federal governments believe is the best way to help our downtrodden fellow man. Over several decades, minorities have been led to look to the government to empower them. The problem is:

Most government programs do not empower people. They actually enslave them.

Why? Well, first, more often than not, the government steals from them their sense of dignity, stamping them as second-class citizens. Then the assistance provided is often the wrong guidance. The result is that many, if not most, government programs actually turn out to be part of the problem instead of the solution. Programs from any agency of the government that do not have at their center a self-help mandate are destined to fail. You can count on it. As a matter of fact, strange as it sounds, many workers even in the corporate world are also enslaved. Corporations of all sizes are notorious for selling employees a program of benefits that, in reality, are often never forthcoming, even though the employee stays with the corporation through thick and thin. This package of benefits becomes a source of fear, the fear that if they leave they will lose something that cannot be replaced.

This fear often causes them to miss real opportunities for higher achievement elsewhere. I have known many men and women who, for fear of losing their so-called benefit package, have completely lost their sense of worth. They stay in a job they have grown to hate. They work for supervisors who berate and mistreat them. Their self-image has been completely destroyed. They simply put in their time as a man condemned to prison would.

Here is the key to avoid these pitfalls.

Do not look to someone else for help.

You have every right to be empowered for success, to build a dynamic self-image. The answer is within you. You are able to achieve without crutches, *government or corporate handouts.*

You have within you the right stuff for success, so empower yourself today. How? By starting right now to change the way you see yourself. Begin right now to see yourself *not as you are but as you want to be.*

It does not matter what you
have or have not done in the past;
what matters is what you are currently thinking.

The fact is:

You are today where your thoughts
have brought you and you are building
your future by the quality of thinking
that you are doing today.

If you tell me your thoughts, I can predict your future. That is what I mean when I say:

To think is to create.

So whenever you are ready, you can choose to change your thinking and as I have said before, if you change your thinking, your world will change.

THE THIRD GREAT SUCCESS SECRET:

Be Committed To The Task; Educate Yourself In The Ways Of Success.

In the first century AD there was a Greek philosopher who wrote a line that has stood the test of time. This man's name was Epictetus and he wrote these few simple but dynamic words:

"Only the educated are free."

That was true in the first century and is true in this century as well. When you decide to commit yourself to being educated in the ways of success, all of your deepest and most intimate thoughts are channeled into a new stream of growth consciousness. The character of your mental and spiritual makeup is going to change and this will affect the remaining aspects of your being: the vocational, the financial, the physical, the family, the social and even your long-range goals.

Here is what Herbert Spencer had to say about continuing to learn:

"Education has for its object the formation of character."

That is true. No matter how small a start you make, good, wholesome success character is going to be formed and the results will be that your attitudes, thoughts, dreams and visions will take on a success nature. You will see yourself in a new light, a healthy, happy and powerful light. I challenge you to begin today. Right now, commit yourself to studying the ways and means of success. Is this not the reason you purchased this book? Well, dig in.

Allow Dr. William James to speak personally to you, "You can literally change your life by changing your thinking." So change your thinking and your world will change and remember this to be successful:

You must be willing, at any given moment, to sacrifice what you are, for what you could become.

I am going to take time out here and preach a little. My subject is that of nature. Now, consider very carefully these following few sentences. They will unlock the door to your developing a powerful, healthy self-image.

"Among the multitude of animals who scamper, fly, burrow and swim around us, man is the only one who is not locked into his environment. His imagination, his reason, his emotional subtlety and his toughness make it possible for him not to just accept the environment but to change it." These few words from *The Ascent of Man* by Jacob Bronowski clearly capture the potential you have to shape the landscape of your own life.

Know this: you *do not* have to accept the *present circumstances of your life*. If you are not happy with what you see, *you can change it*.

How can you change it?

- By imagination

- By reason

- By emotional subtlety

- By toughness

You have these four virtues within you, which you can use to educate yourself in the ways of success.

First: **You possess the power of imagination.**

By thinking and speaking, you can imagine yourself to be different and different you become. It was Wallace Stevens who wrote:

> **"In the world of words, the imagination**
> **is one of the forces of nature."**

That is high praise. The imagination is like the fierce wind, hail and lightning. The imagination is a power equal to or beyond anything, we know in nature. Imagination changes men. With a creative imagination, focusing on the clean, the pure, the powerful and the positive, you will automatically draw into yourself those characteristics of the life of success. What a resource. You will never run out of imagination, because every time you use it, your imagination grows and multiplies. It is true:

> **The more you use your imagination,**
> **the more it replenishes itself.**

Second: **You have the ability to reason.**

Here is another way to express this thought:

> **You are the answer to your own questions.**

You can reason what you must do to become successful. You can gain the education whereby you will apply the principle of reason to your goals. Here again you see the value of creating for yourself specific, concrete, crystallized goals.

Third: **Once you have your specific goals, you will have emotional subtlety.**

With emotional subtlety, you will feel fired up, ready to hit the ground running. Your life will take on a whole new meaning. Food will taste better, songs will sound better and on the inside you will even feel better.

Fourth: **You will have a mental and physical toughness you have never known.**

When your imagination is fixed on a specific goal and you have used your ability to reason your way though the obstacles before you, your emotional batteries will be fully charged and you will be able to tap into a newly discovered mental and physical toughness. You will not be sidelined by the daily turbulence that might otherwise take you out of the game.

THE FOURTH GREAT SUCCESS SECRET:
Develop A Passion For Your Goals And Life.

You will find that people on target to reach their goals have a burning passion to see their dreams come true. By continually keeping their mind fixed on their goals, over time, this passion builds and releases energy for action, for climbing, building, constantly moving forward to the high and lofty place of success, honor and peace of mind.

I must be careful here at this juncture. When I speak of passion and the release of it into your life, I'm not speaking of enthusiasm. One can be *enthusiastic* and not be *passionate*. When I speak of passion, I speak of a quality of life that glows from the lamp of love, faith, determination and enthusiasm.

It is when all four of these emotions begin pouring out of you toward the fulfillment of your goals that passion is born. Passion conquers problems. Passion keeps on keeping on. With passion at your side, your fears and doubts are rebuked. You see only the finish line of completing all of your goals.

In reviewing these four great concepts to building a powerful, healthy self-image, notice how each of them dovetails to the other, creating, if you will, a master plan for developing within you a great feeling of confidence that you are someone very special.

One: *Only shallow men believe in luck.*

Two: *Always demand of yourself a spirit of self-help.*

Three: *Educate yourself in the ways of success.*

Four: *Develop a passion for your goals and life.*

Each of the four concepts taken alone is not difficult to understand or even master. Yet when all four of these success concepts are in place in your life, you will change. If your image heretofore has been less than what you want it to be, you will come to see yourself in a new light. In addition, if you have always had a great image of yourself, adopt these four concepts and it will even be greater.

This is not a sleight-of-hand trick wherein you fool yourself. This is one of the success laws of the universe. You are what you think about. Therefore you can change the quality of your life by changing the quality of your thinking. A poor self-image is self-induced. However, a confident self-image is also self-induced. It all begins and ends in the thinking processes of your own mind.

I now share with you what I believe is one of the greatest statements ever made with respect to seeing yourself and your situations in a positive, forthright manner. These few words from Ralph Waldo Emerson speak a truth and a challenge that everyone should hear and take to heart.

"All that Adam had, all that Caesar could,
you have and can do.
Build, therefore, your own world."

Emerson saw right through to the heart of the matter. He knew three vital truths about all men. First, the stuff Adam and Caesar are made of, you are made of. Now, it is true that all do not start at the same gate, yet all do start. Adam and Caesar had different ideas and dreams than you but your ideas and dreams are just as valid as far as the ability to dream and turn dreams into reality, to build for yourself a life of success.

Adam and Caesar also experienced the negatives of life. You are not alone in this struggle. Their potential to succeed rests at this moment in you. They wrote their life histories with the same pen that is now in your hand.

Times have changed,
but people's ability to achieve,
to do more, to have more and
to become more remains the same.

Their knowledge is different from your knowledge but the basic keys that create success are exactly the same for modern man as for ancient man. This will never change.

Secondly, you have the complete and full liberty for success and prosperity. Yes, Success is your birthright, failure your option. The key to why America is truly the land of opportunity is the precious liberty that exists in this country. Think about it. There are no border guards to stop you as you move from state to state. There are no limits to how wealthy you can become. You can build your house where you wish and even expect service from the city and state agencies protecting your freedom. James Otis, one of the early promoters of liberty in this country, had as his motto these immortal words:

"Where liberty is, there is my country."

I really appreciate his commitment and work to ensure that every person in this nation was free and at liberty to seek success and prosperity. You know what? You are one of those persons. No people in the history of civilization have been given such full and complete liberty as the citizens of the United States of America. Each year people place themselves in grave danger in order to reach our shores, hoping to live in the land of the free. In short, there is no nation such as ours. What Adam and Caesar had you have. In fact, you have even more.

Thirdly, build!

Make it happen! Emerson was even more specific. He was saying since you have what Adam and Caesar had and can do anything equal to what they could do, then by all means build the kind of world that will make you happy.

Emerson knew a tremendous secret about you. Your world, the real world, is in your mind. Whatever you desire the most, if you persist, in time that painting appears on the canvas of reality. It is your choice. You can fashion a world of despair or of delight, a world of beauty or of brutish sights and sounds. Today you become the master painter. The strokes of the brush are commanded by the inner view that you have of yourself, of your life and of your future. I have said it before but I will say it again, because it is true for me, for others and yes, for you, too. It is absolutely true:

To think is to create.

It was Thomas Mann who wrote:

"Order and simplification are the first steps toward the mastery of a subject."

By reading this chapter, you are simplifying and dealing with the goal of building a powerful, healthy self-image.

Do you see that it all begins to take place first in your mind? So take hold of these concepts and activities and begin the secret steps of building an image of yourself that will lead you to the *Richer Life*. Once you capture the picture on the inside, that is, in your mind, your whole being will begin to change. Success will not seem as distant as it was before.

One last thought: whatever it takes to develop a powerful, healthy self-image, it will be worth it. Let me encourage you to start right now. Start where you are; do not delay.

The great philosopher Plato spoke these words of wisdom:

"The beginning is the most important part of the work."

I have given you four dynamic *Richer Life* concepts for building a powerful, healthy self-image. This is your beginning. Throw yourself into this work. Do not allow anyone or anything to interrupt or interfere. *Plan* your *work*; then *work* your *plan*. Change will not appear overnight. However, I promise you it will appear.

This is the law. You will become what you think about. I am truly excited for you. I know that you are going to make several important discoveries about yourself in the near future. I wish I could be there with you, to watch your new self-image develop. Remember it all begins and ends in the thinking processes of your own mind.

Christopher Morley once wrote:

"There is only one success—to be able to spend your life in your own way."

Get ready. With your new powerful healthy self-image that is exactly what is going to happen to you. Welcome to a new life; a life of hope, achievement and success. Welcome to the *Richer Life*.

We Have The Power
To Shape Our Environment.

Rick C. Ernst

Chapter Ten

GETTING ORGANIZED FOR SUCCESS

I n this chapter I will provide you the resources to organize your life in such a way that success will surely follow. I have discovered five great success axioms that really work and I am excited to share them with you. Dr. Ira North, an outstanding minister and communication teacher, once said:

"If you are organized
you can make water run uphill."

One thing you quickly notice about successful people is that they have a certain fluidity in their lives, as opposed to the majority of people who seem to go through life in a herky-jerky fashion.

Successful people always seem to be an inch or two off the ground. The bumps and bruises that sideline the unsuccessful have little or no effect on these success-oriented, highly organized achievers. They seem to glide across the landscape of life. They are organized for success and success happens for them. Success can happen to you also. My objective in this chapter is to prepare you to be ready when the next ship of opportunity sails in.

There are five secret success axioms to study as we begin to organize your life and work for accomplishment and success. Each of these five great ideas represents a vital key to organizing yourself and each idea requires your concentrated effort. I will introduce each of these secret success axioms and then I will discuss their value one idea at a time.

Here are the five secret success axioms.

One: Define the success you envision.

Two: Before you clean up, as in making money, you need to clear out.

Three: Your plans must include happiness and peace of mind.

Four: Procrastination is a real enemy.

Five: Do not be afraid of things others call impossible.

THE FIRST SECRET SUCCESS AXIOM:
Define The Success You Envision.

A great intellect who has visited us before in this book, Thomas Mann, has an great idea for you that is vital to your understanding of how to organize your life and work for success:

> *"Order and simplification are
> the first steps toward the mastery of
> a subject. The actual enemy is the unknown."*

Mann presents three ideas worthy of our consideration. One:

> *You must create order in your life
> if you expect to be successful.*

Make no mistake about it. Thomas Mann is suggesting that your life as a whole must have an order to it, not that every single aspect of your life must be in order.

He suggests that you get a grip on your life by defining the success you envision. Bring a general order to your life so you can begin the process of working on specific issues leading to success. This will be a decisive moment in your life. Two Points need to be made about this step to bring order to your life. One: *In decision making the truth is, more is lost by indecision than wrong decision.* Two: *It is more important to do the right thing than it is to do things right.*

The point is that bringing overall order into your life may require you to make some painful decisions. If that is true, make them and when making them, do the right thing. Do not try to shortcut the success process. Do not slide. Be firm. Define the success you envision. Then, position yourself to be ready when positive opportunities present themselves. In addition to bringing order to your life, Mann also suggests:

You must simplify your life.

If you just look around, you will find most people have too much needless activity in their life. They have not yet learned to say *no* to projects that they are not interested in or really do not want to do.

It does not take long to get one's life totally immersed in activities that bring little or no success results and happiness. Therefore, you must begin to simplify your life. As this chapter unfolds, you will discover a great number of exciting ways to accomplish that feat. Mann goes on to suggest:

Your real enemy is the unknown.

He is right. I can tell you this for sure: no matter what the situation, once you know the extent of the problems you face, you will actually feel a sense of relief. At least you know where you are. Once you know where you are, you can get to where you want to go.

Bringing a sense of order to your life, plus simplifying what you can, will often make known the unknown. Instead of being fearful or unsure of your next move, you can now begin to define the success you envision. You can start to set those priorities for your life that will bring enthusiasm and determination into play. When I say to you that you must define the success you envision, I am saying you must develop specific goals for your life. Sound familiar? Goal setting is the first step to success, whether you are getting organized or actively at work. It is amazing how many opportunities will surface in your life once you are focused and organized. Over the years, I have seen people turn their entire lives around in just a few days, simply by defining what they want out of life and setting forth a game plan to achieve those goals. When you are ready, you can do the same. Yes, it is very important that you define exactly what your view of success is. Without a doubt, it is the first bold step to organizing your life for success.

The Second Secret Success Axiom:
Before You Clean Up, As In Making Money, Clear Out.

Watching people as I have, as well as working with them in one-on-one coaching sessions and my live events, I can relate one clear fact: *most people's lives are cluttered with lost opportunities, fragmented relationships and no system of processing the opportunities that come their way.* Often I hear people say "My life is a mess," and they are right. However, before you can clean up, you often have to clear out. Here are five great ideas that will help you:

Begin to organize your life with a cleanup perspective.

One: *Clutter is clutter:*

You have to face the facts about Clutter. Call it what you will but clutter is clutter and as such, must be cleared out. If your financial condition permits, you will move along the highway to success much faster if you can discard almost everything that reminds you of your past life and purchase a totally new look for yourself.

In the past I have moved into new offices. I have even sold my home and purchased a new one. I have on more than one occasion even moved to another state. Whatever it takes, *clear out the clutter* and get rid of everything that reminds you of past failures. Sometimes it is hard to do but it must be done.

Two: **Learn to let go.**

This point is not so much about physical clutter as it is about your personal life and relationships. You may need to make a conscious effort to let go of the past and those people associated with it.

Remember this:

**The past is the past. The past lives in you,
but you do not have to live in the past.**

Just because something in your past is negative, that is no reason to drag it around with you. You are now getting organized for success, not for failure. So let these past failures and setbacks go. See them for what they are. Learn from them if you can but let them go.

I want to take just a moment longer here because this point needs to be amplified. All experts would agree that one of the greatest hindrances to success is a continuing negative relationship. Perhaps you have been in a relationship in the past that was full of disappointment and personal grief or maybe even abuse of some sort. If so, you must find a way to let those memories go.

To continue to harbor and dwell upon these negative thoughts is an exercise in futility. Or perhaps you have had a false start in your career and things did not work out as you wished. Again, learn from this experience all that you can but above all, deal with it and let the negative memories go. They cannot help you, only hinder you. Learn to let go. Have the courage of your convictions. *Clear out and then you can clean up.*

Three: **Sometimes less is more.**

When you analyze the way most successful people live, they live a streamlined life. Yes, successful people have far less clutter and because of that, more energy. They end up with more money, time, happiness and more often, they have fewer acquaintances but they experience less stress. They have discovered that *less can be more.* This is not to say that these successful people have ceased their pursuit of success, happiness and prosperity—not at all.

It does mean, however, that they have put their life in proper perspective. They realize that chasing things can get out of hand and that less can actually be more.

Four: **When something new arrives, discard something old.**

This is a great rule for your home as well as the office. When something new arrives, find something old that can be discarded. You will find any number of items to which this rule will apply: everything from clothes to magazines, household items to office purchases. It is simple. *When something new arrives, discard something old.*

Five: **Have a place for everything and have everything in its place.**

Nothing is as frustrating and as detrimental to good positive energy as attempting to find something that has been misplaced. Similarly, having an organized work area speaks volumes about you as a person. I have seen exceptions to the rule but it was just that, an exception. The rule is:

> **A cluttered workspace
> testifies to a cluttered mind.**

The other side of this coin is that *order breeds good habits.* Just the very activity of creating a place for everything at work, at home, in the garage, will automatically create in your mind a sense of accomplishment and order. Now you are ready to achieve greater success than ever before.

There you have them: five great ideas to help you organize your work and your life. Before you can clean up, as in making money, becoming a success, you often have to clear out of your life the clutter, the negative attitudes, the destructive negative relationships. Whatever it takes, just do it! Get organized for success and success will surely follow.

> ## THE THIRD SECRET SUCCESS AXIOM:
> ### Include Happiness And Peace Of Mind In Your Success Plan.

This may sound strange but it is true, as a life success coach I know many people and most others would call them *very successful people.* Yet these so-called *successful people* are *not* happy with their lives and have very little peace of mind.

Believe me when I say; "*happiness and peace of mind must be apart of your overall plan, they do not just automatically follow success.*"

Here are four ideas that will help you to include happiness in your quest for success, as well as ensure your daily peace of mind.

One: ***Be physically ready to succeed.***

With few exceptions, becoming successful will *require 110 percent from your work effort.* Often people are not in physical shape to concentrate, to be intense about success. To be blunt, they wear out; grow despondent, attempt shortcuts and soon their entire plan of action falls apart.

To avoid being caught in this trap, you will want to eat a proper diet, develop a plan for daily exercise and, of utmost importance, find some type of fun recreational activity. In short, get yourself in good physical shape. It is a fact; you will need every ounce of energy you can muster as you climb the ladder of success.

Two: ***Do not overdo it.***

In their exuberance to get organized as quickly as possible, many people throw themselves into their work and, even if they are in relatively good shape, overdo a good thing. At moments like this, it is easy to become discouraged, disillusioned, even burned out and then negativity creeps in. So instead, lay out a schedule: plan your work and then work your plan. The end result is to enjoy yourself as you work.

That is not to say that you will not occasionally have a rough day or even week. But overall, if you are not experiencing good times, personal growth and happiness, something is wrong. Or to say it another way: if you are experiencing stress most of the time, you are doing it wrong.

The truth of the matter is you were designed for *success*. To fail is not *natural*. It is *normal* for many people but that does not make it *natural*. That is why failure feels so bad.

Three: **Keep your eye on the prize.**

The goal of getting organized for success is not the prize but the preparation to win the prize. So keep your eye on your goals. This will help you persist in your organizational efforts. Some days it may seem as if your headway is totally blocked. On these days, remember:

> **You cannot do everything at once,**
> **but you can do something at once.**

Keep your eye on the prize. Push forward, even if it seems fruitless. Your victory will come. I promise you that your organizational efforts will pay off. Success will follow.

Four: **Balance is the key to peace of mind.**

Yes, having your life in balance or, I could say, moderation is the balancing weight of your life. This is why setting goals in every area of your life is so important. I challenge you to include happiness and peace of mind in your success plan at all times. Edwin Bliss makes a point to consider:

> **"There is a difference between striving**
> **for excellence and striving for perfection.**

The first is obtainable, gratifying and healthy.

The second is unattainable, frustrating, and neurotic. It is also a terrible waste of time."

The key here is that if you concentrate on becoming a man or woman of excellence, your heart will lead you to the success you desire. Fulfillment, personal growth, happiness and peace of mind will be exciting by-products of your efforts. If you think you have to be perfect in whatever you do, frustration and discouragement will sweep through your body and happiness and certainly peace of mind, will be a distant wish.

THE FOURTH SECRET SUCCESS AXIOM:
Remind Yourself Daily That Procrastination Is A Real And Present Enemy.

I am confident of this fact: *procrastination is the single greatest activity of failure you will ever encounter.* I appreciate what Donald Marquis once wrote about procrastination:

"Procrastination is the art of keeping up with yesterday."

When procrastination is in your life, you end up a day late and a dollar short. You never quite get there. As a result, you never get organized, your time is wasted and others who are busy every day with the real priorities of their lives move ahead of you. William Shakespeare wrote:

"A slothful person will find his pillow hard."

Shakespeare was right. Not only do you fail in your work habits when you procrastinate but at night when you finally lie down, your conscience will prick you, guilt will rise and sleep will not come. Your pillow, which should be soft and comfortable, will seem hard and the good night's rest you need will elude you. This is the payoff for procrastination. There is no doubt about it; *procrastination is a real and present enemy.* Anytime procrastination rears its ugly head in your life, know it for what it is, *an enemy.* Push it aside by beginning immediately to do what needs to be done. Force yourself to tackle the job at hand. Soon you will develop the habit of success and procrastination will be forced out of your life.

> ## THE FIFTH SECRET SUCCESS AXIOM:
> ### Do Not Be Afraid Of Things Others Call Impossible.

So many people are quick to put a label on difficult projects, saying the dreaded words "That's impossible." After saying, "That's impossible," rarely will this person attempt to solve the problem or pursue the project until they become successful.

When I was a child, my father often told me that saying things like *"I can't," "It's too hard,"* or *"It's impossible"* was losers' talk. Here is how he would express it:

"A winner says it may be difficult but it's possible."

Joe Darion wrote the following lyrics, which I think give great insight as to how to conduct your life to be successful:

"To dream the impossible dream, to reach the unreachable star."

This is how we were meant to live. Yes, things may be *difficult* but they are not *impossible.* What really is the difference between the *possible* and the *impossible?* Let Tommy Lasorda, the baseball manager, tell you:

"The difference between the possible and the impossible lies in your determination."

Does that fit somewhere in your life right now? Read the idea again. That is the key. Determination is in a winner's attitude. If you are determined, you will find a way. You may have to go the extra mile, working harder than you ever worked before but if you keep at it the possibilities for success are endless.

Back in the sixteenth century, John Haywood wrote a book entitled *Proverbs*. One of the proverbs is especially relevant.

"Nothing is impossible to a willing heart."

Now that is a great affirmation! The way I see it is that the impossible becomes possible the moment we become willing to search for the solution to the challenge before us.

The term *willing heart* means, at least to me, that I am willing to work with every ounce of my physical, emotional, mental and spiritual energy. I refuse to quit. I refuse to be pushed aside. I refuse to accept anything less than success. That is a willing heart. The great French general Napoleon Bonaparte was an unbeatable and unstoppable warrior. He taught a slogan to his junior officers and men in the field:

"Impossible is not a French word."

You can imagine the success you could acquire if you did not allow the word *impossible* to be used by yourself and others who work with you. Napoleon simply refused to allow the word impossible to be a part of a French soldier's vocabulary.

However, of all the ideas, proverbs and philosophical statements about the word impossible and the negative results that come from thinking that things are impossible, the all-time best attitude belongs to the United States Air Force. When it comes to describing how to deal with the word impossible, the Air Force says:

"The difficult we do immediately;
the impossible takes a little while longer."

Now, that is a great attitude. I am constantly amazed at the way people react to challenges and the results that flow forth in their lives. There have been a few times in the past when I have thought to myself, "There is no way this person is going to be successful at what they are attempting to do." However, after a while I discovered I was totally wrong. They were succeeding at the very thing, which I believed they would fail. How could I have been so wrong?

It is simple. I was judging their idea. I did not take into account their faith in themselves, their total commitment, the clarity of their goals and the dynamics of their plan of action.

It is this hidden-away part of a person, the part we never see, this place where organization for success takes place and where the attitudes develop, that does not quake in fear when someone says, *"That's impossible."*

Here, in the final pages of this chapter, I want to take a moment to commend you for staying with me thus far in this book. Others, no doubt, have quit some chapters ago and have returned to their old ways of thinking. But you have decided you want a better life for yourself and that tells me you are on your way.

Once you are organized, you will have purpose. That is what organizing for success is all about. You are saying to the world: *"Move over; give me some room. I am ready and here I come, like it or not."* Guess what? The world moves over. The door to success opens up. You are welcomed. I know this firsthand: there is always room at the top for one more.

Here is the final admonition. Remember this above all, once you make up your mind that you are going to get organized for success and strive for the very highest position on the ladder of success, at this point the die is cast. There can be no looking back. You may have to sail uncharted seas. You may have to find new friends. You may not be understood by those who were used to the old you. Emerson wrote:

"It's a luxury to be understood."

He is right. Those friends, acquaintances and even loved ones were comfortable with the old you. The new you may be far more difficult to figure out. The old you was satisfied with the status quo. The new you demands change. Old habits die hard and change is never easy. But you will do it.

With your new attitude toward getting organized for success, your destiny is one of fulfillment, accomplishment, personal growth, happiness, peace of mind and purpose. Do you know why I am so certain of your success? I will tell you by sharing a statement from Washington Irving:

"Great minds have purposes;
others have wishes."

That is so true. When it comes down to it, the real difference between people is *purpose*. A strong sense of purpose can accomplish anything. *Impossible* is ruled out. All options are open.

Now your *purpose* is to get organized for success. In doing so, your goals and dreams will be clear, specific, filled with honest ambition and *purpose*.

In eternity past, before God created the world, His desire was to make the world in such a way that everything would have a purpose and He did. There is nothing present in our world that does not have a purpose, including *you*.

Sometimes we might not understand how it all works but everything and everyone has a purpose. And, I might add,

You were given life for a grand purpose.

The exciting part is you have the liberty at any moment to say,

"I am now ready
to fulfill my purpose."

As you follow these five success axioms to organizing yourself for success, your *purpose* will shine forth, your star of destiny will rise.

Success will come and along with it the happiness, joy and the peace of mind of a fulfilled, *Richer Life*.

Chapter Eleven

OVERCOMING STRESS AND MANAGING PERSONAL CONFLICT

I realize that in this chapter I am tackling one of the greatest negatives and one of the crippling forces of our society. It seems that the vast majority of people will have to deal with stress in virtually all areas of their lives.

In times past, I too was held hostage by this great enemy that keeps so many people from success, prosperity, happiness and for sure, peace of mind. I have divided this chapter into three specific areas.

One: Defining what stress is and how it affects us.

Two: Providing you with seven simple, effective ways to reduce and even eliminate stress from your life.

Three: Developing a dynamic stress-free philosophy.

The first concept to understanding and handling stress is to define and relate how it affects people. Before I do this, I want to show you the effects of stress as described by the medical community.

Today many researchers believe that as high as 75 percent of medical complaints are stress-related. A recent University of Tennessee study discovered that approximately 50 percent of all hospital admissions could be corrected by changes in lifestyles that would reduce stress.

These examples provide a reason to believe those who claim that the twenty-first century is the age of anxiety. Based on the next example, I too have come to believe this.

Consider these facts: each year in America, doctors dispense over *five million* prescriptions for tranquilizers, *three million* prescriptions for amphetamines and *five billion* prescriptions for barbiturates. This accounts for only three of the legal drugs designed to combat stress, not to mention the millions upon millions of dollars in illegal drugs flowing into our communities on a daily basis.

What is this thing we call stress? How does it find its way into our mental and emotional systems? A dictionary definition of the word *stress* provides insight as to just what stress does inside of our bodies. Here's how Webster's dictionary describes a stressful situation:

Stress is the result of the action or effect of force exerted within or upon something.

Usually when you think of something under pressure, strain or tension, such as the stress put on a bridge by a heavily loaded truck. We speak of the stress factor as being the pressure or the weight that could cause the bridge to fail.

So it is in your life. When you internalize outside negative situations, you actually put a heavy load on your mental and emotional system. Over time, as more and more negativity and stress-laden problems build up, the greater the danger of some sort of a breakdown be it mental, physical or even spiritual.

The effects are emotional illness, physical disorders, loss of concentration, lack of energy, headaches, negative attitude, angered spirit, a feeling of sadness, a sense of being out of touch or out of control and high blood pressure. In fact the effects of stress seem to be unending.

One fact is certain: stress can be as damaging as disease caused by viruses, for stress seems to spread through the entire body, affecting every aspect of our being. The good news is that there is a complete cure for stress.

However, the cure does not happen overnight but it will happen. There is also a vital payoff; you will once again take control of your life by determining what creates stress for you. Then you can avoid these negative stressful situations. We must recognize that not all stress is negative or harmful. Some stress actually supercharges your success system, releasing your creative powers of faith and enthusiasm. Positive stress and positive challenges can cause you to stretch into a new dimension of life.

All right, enough said about what stress is. Let us now turn to seven simple steps to reduce and even eliminate negative stress.

These seven steps may seem familiar yet they are truly the basis of stress reduction. You will do well to incorporate them into your thinking process.

STEP NUMBER ONE:
Learn To Laugh—Especially At Yourself.

Laughter is always good medicine. In Judeo-Christian literature we are told, "There is a time to weep and a time to laugh." When you grow to the point that you can laugh at your mistakes, at your less-than-best decisions, your life will begin to become stress-free.

Robert Allen wrote on this point:

*"Don't let the opinions of
the average man sway you.*

*Dream and he thinks you're crazy.
Succeed and he thinks you're lucky.*

Acquire wealth and he thinks
you're greedy. Pay no attention.
He simply doesn't understand."

Each one of the above statements is true. When you are striving for success, prosperity and financial independence and someone says something derogatory, simply smile and go on. Open up your mouth and laugh your way to success.

You have heard the expression, "He is laughing all the way to the bank." Well, that is someone who has learned to laugh when others tried to put him down. Now his reward is evident. His laughter has paid off.

STEP NUMBER TWO:
Express Your Love On A Daily Basis.

It goes without saying that you must first express love to yourself, not in an egotistical manner but simply as an expression that you honor who you are, a person of vitality, purpose, promise and character. When you make a commitment to express your love to others, two exciting things begin to happen. One, expressing love to others is like planting a seed. You will experience a multiplied harvest of love flowing back into your life. Second, you are a true blessing to other people. Pay close attention to this:

The human spirit craves
recognition. No award compares
with the power of verbal recognition.

This illustration is proven over and over again. Take the night of the Oscars in Hollywood. The movie stars who win those coveted awards could care less about the statue itself. It is the recognition of their work by their peers that really counts and is remembered.

When you express your recognition and love to others, you lift them in body and spirit. And, in addition to that, they accept your love and will respond by being the type of person you hope them to become. The philosopher Goethe said it best:

*"Treat people as though they
were what they ought to be and you
help them become what they are capable of being."*

That is the way love works. Believe me on this: love always works. The response to your love may not be immediate but, in time, love will complete its task. Change will be evident. For sure, some people are harder to love than others are. But remember:

*A leader sees people for the
potential they have, not the way they are.*

STEP NUMBER THREE:
Simplify Your Life.

A great amount of stress is found in the lives of those whose possessions possess them. I would add that massive debt usually accompanies this lifestyle and, over time, it takes its toll.

When I suggest that you keep your life simple, I am only asking that you follow faithfully the basic steps to prosperity and happiness. Use your money management system we talked about in Chapter Eight and in so doing stick to your plan.

In addition, practice delayed gratification. Be practical about your expenditures. Do not get trapped into *keeping up with the Joneses*. Follow your own star. Think your own thoughts. Do not clutter up your life with all kinds of things and so-called important possessions. Remember the rule:

*Always be bigger
than your possessions.*

At this point I can almost hear someone saying, "Obviously you don't understand my life. My life is already cluttered up; in fact it's a mess.

I'm head-over-heels in debt. My income is insufficient. My job is even at risk. 'Simple,' you say. My life is anything but simple. You don't have my life. How could you understand where I am?" If that person is you, I am going to be brutally frank here. Yes, I do understand. That is why I have written this book. Carefully consider these next twenty-one words. Do you want to escape from the life you are living? Then know this:

> *Nothing is impossible. There are ways that lead to everything; and if you have sufficient will, you shall have sufficient means.*

You may say "Yes but I don't have any willpower. My hope is all gone. It's as if I'm circling the drain." Let me ask you to do this. I know you can do this. Everyone can do this. *Are you willing to be willing?*

Think about it. Are you? If you are, I am telling you that you can start right there. And starting there, if you keep reading this book, you will soon renew yourself. You will develop a new strategy and most importantly, you will learn to never give in or give up.

STEP NUMBER FOUR:
Stay Positive About Your Health.

Sometimes stress has a way of creating ill health and then it compounds itself by the negativity it produces. At times illness may be a part of this life. The challenge for you is twofold.

One: *Take care of your body. Eat right. Get plenty of rest. Exercise; treat your body as the important entity it is.*

Two: *Stay positive about your life.*

Consider these words of wisdom from one who had seen more sickness than almost anyone you can think of. I am speaking, of course, of Mother Teresa:

"Life is an opportunity.
Benefit from it."

Wow! What a positive attitude! You see, even illness has its own special rewards. Watch for them. Learn to benefit from each moment of your life.

STEP NUMBER FIVE:
You Are In Control of Your Health.
Be Optimistic.

This point tends to overlap the fourth step, yet it is different. If you are taking the best care of your body you can, if you are seeing to it that your food, your rest, your exercise fit a consistent, healthy pattern, then most of the time your body will respond in a happy, healthy manner. So be optimistic. However, should illness come into your life, treat it as an obstacle. Of course, an obstacle is not the end; it is a new beginning. In doing so, *before* you do get ill, set in your mind that you will profit from an illness. What I mean is, if and when an illness comes your way, while you are ill; ask yourself, *"what can I learn from this illness?"* Then begin to think, *how and whom can I serve during and after my illness?*

I recognize that serious illness leaves some people permanently disabled. Yet the truth remains, *you are in control of your life as long as you control your thoughts.*

Being optimistic is a choice you can make. It is an idea, an idea you can live your life by. Without exception, if you look hard enough, you will always be able to find some way or someone who can benefit from your illness. Remember:

Our service to others
is the rent we pay for the space
we occupy on Earth.

STEP NUMBER SIX:

Everyday Speak To Yourself About The Positive Things That Are Happening In Your Life.

This is a powerful, positive method to awaken every pore and corpuscle in your body. Remind yourself daily of your aspirations. As Robert Browning stated:

"Our aspirations are our possibilities."

When you aspire to achieve success, reminding yourself each day of the positive things that are happening in your life, you will soon see possibilities in every idea, activity and thought. It is right to be the best you can be. It is honorable and virtuous to demand of yourself a life formed around excellence, a strong moral character, a hungering and a drive for the best life possible.

If you are willing, you can fight stress and I might add you can win. You were designed to be a winner, not a loser. You are the crowning of all of God's creation. So set forth a plan of action, follow through and full and lasting success will be yours. This is your birthright: to be your best is first a gift to yourself and second, to him who created you and equipped you for success and excellence.

I promise you this, if you think of success in these terms, the stress and strains of life will appear differently to you. You will see yourself as the valued human being you really are.

STEP NUMBER SEVEN:

Constantly Review Your Goals And Priorities. Do Not Get In Over Your Head.

At first blush, this may sound like a contradiction to other coaching I have given you but it is not. By all means set challenging goals for yourself, be a dreamer, be everything you can be but, above all, constantly review your goals and priorities. Do not get into more than you can handle.

There is a philosophy that says, "If you bite off more than you can chew, just chew it anyway." I usually agree with that kind of thinking but on this issue, I realize not everyone has the same mental and emotional makeup.

Here is the key: if you are not having fun on a daily basis, not being fulfilled, it is not worth it. Yes, I say, stretch yourself, reach for goals beyond your grasp but do not overload your capacity to handle events or try to move in a certain direction too fast. Dream to walk around the world, if you choose but make sure your action plan has you taking each step one at a time. While on your journey, if you decide to run instead of walk, that is okay too but you must still make sure you are putting one foot in front of the other. Otherwise you could stumble.

Now you have the seven dynamic concepts for handling the stress and strain that comes with striving to be the best you can be. Let us now look at the philosophy of understanding *self* as it relates to stress and the pursuit of success.

There are three thoughts that I want you to consider, great ideas that I have used for years, ideas that can also work for you! As you use these ideas, the stress of your life will diminish. You will feel great about yourself, your life, your goals and your future. The first philosophical thought:

> *"Success is not measured by what*
> *a man accomplishes but rather by*
> *the opposition he has encountered*
> *and the courage he maintained during*
> *his struggle against overwhelming odds."*

This compelling statement is from Charles Lindbergh, a man who dared the impossible, the first transoceanic crossing of the Atlantic by air. As Lindbergh was over the ocean, flying at night, unsure of his fuel consumption, he fought the cold, lack of sleep and exhaustion. His personal courage was all that kept him together, the unshakeable belief in man's ability to achieve in spite of trying circumstances. So it is with you. Have the courage of your convictions. Stand firm. Always press forward. I have found in my life that if I persevere, in time success is assured. I rest on that faith. I maintain that faith. I live by that faith and so can you.

The second thought:

Your happiness or misery depends on your disposition, not your circumstances.

That is the key. Webster's dictionary defines *disposition* as a prevailing tendency, mood or inclination. Disposition is our temperamental makeup. So be disposed toward the positive. Concentrate on the positive. Be active in the positive. Rest in the positive and decide this very moment, to always think positive.

Stop and think about it. Stress begins in the conscious mind. Then it quickly links up with the emotional side of your life and when fed by continual negative thoughts, it develops into the full-blown conditions of stress. You can eliminate all this by remembering that even in your worst misery, a seed of equal or greater positive benefit can be harvested.

As Zig Ziglar says:

"Your attitude determines your altitude."

You can experience a continuing mental high by concentrating on the development of a positive disposition. It is your choice. You can be negative or you can be positive. No one can decide for you. You must make that decision. I challenge you to decide today.

Decide right now to let your mood swing always be up, not down, always rest in the positive, not the negative. I would like to leave this point here and just say that all you have to do is keep thinking positive and everything will be okay. But to do this would be short-sighted. As with many things, life's problems come in all sizes small, medium, large and extra-large. However, sometimes life brings an oversized problem, size XXL.

Now, I am not talking about those problems that are just big inconveniences or disappointments. I am talking about those giant-sized problems that are so great they knock you flat as a pancake.

A loss or hurt, of such proportion that it sucks the life right out of your body, something that cuts so deep you cannot see any way of going on or maybe you do not even want to. I am talking about those kinds of adversities in life that are devastating.

I have coached many people who, for a variety of reasons, were completely shattered over something or someone. Almost without exception during that time, none of them had a positive disposition, even though before many of them were very positive people. Some even said they wanted to be positive but could not because they were completely devastated. When something hits you this hard, you can temporarily lose your ability to feel and think positive. However, remember, I said earlier regardless of what happens you can always choose to think positive or negative. Well, that is still true.

The problem is when you are devastated, sometimes it is hard, to find something positive to turn your thinking toward. It is at this time that you need a safety net.

For a safety net to be usable and valuable, it must be prepared in advance. I am about to give you a safety net. This safety net is your fallback. It is where you can gather your thoughts, find rest for your racing mind and actually begin the healing process from the devastation. This faith safety net is not some new philosophy or mental discipline. It is actually an exercise of your faith.

When your positive feelings and attitude have been completely crushed to the ground by some devastating act, in these times all you have left is your faith. This faith axiom or as I call it, a faith safety net, is given to us in the handbook of life. Of course I am referring to the Holy Scriptures. In fact, this faith safety net is actually the centerpiece of the New Testament.

This is where, when you have been knocked back to ground zero, you can rest, collect your breath and then start to move forward again. I am speaking of Romans 8:28–29. Here is your safety net in action.

> *And we know that all in things*
> *God works for the good of those who love Him,*
> *who have been called according to his purpose.*
>
> *For those whom He foreknew, He also*
> *predestined to be conformed to the likeness of His son...*

Some day you may need a safety net. I have always found this to be a safe haven for me.

The third thought:

> *You burn three times more energy*
> *when you are upset and negative*
> *than when you are relaxed and positive.*

Here again you have positive proof that your attitude toward yourself, your dreams and aspirations will determine your results.

The bottom line: You have choices you can make every day, every hour and every moment to shape your circumstances and dictate your future. Now you have the *Richer Life Secrets* to overcoming stress and managing personal conflict, seven simple but dynamic steps to eliminating stress from your life. Here they are again.

One: Learn to laugh at yourself.

Two: Express your love on a daily basis.

Three: Simplify your life.

Four: Stay positive about your health.

Five: Take control of your health and food intake.

Six: Speak to yourself daily about the positive things that are happening in your life.

Seven: Stay abreast of your goals and priorities; do not get in over your head.

If you adopt these seven proven steps, you will never again worry about stress. You will move straight forward, one step at a time, on to success and the fulfillment of all your dreams. You will in fact be living the *Richer Life*.

Change Your Thinking and
Your World Will Change.

Rick C. Ernst

CHAPTER

TWELVE

POSITIVE SELF-ESTEEM: THE AXIOM OF PERSONAL HAPPINESS AND SUCCESS

This is an insightful and very important, life-changing chapter. Therefore, I approach it with the greatest care. I certainly know the value of positive self-esteem and I also know the building blocks necessary to produce greater self-esteem; after this chapter, so will you.

Over the years, I have observed countless individuals struggling with the process of attaining greater self-esteem. Their struggle was in part because they did not know the secrets of developing positive self-esteem. This will not be so in your case. This, as I said, is a life-changing chapter.

I am confident that I can lead you into a greater understanding of how to increase your positive self-esteem. Once this is accomplished, you will enjoy more success and happiness. I have decided, however, not to follow the usual plan that most psychologists would prescribe.

As we travel though this subject, I will *not* ask you to identify your weaknesses and strengths. Neither will I ask you how you see yourself, nor how you think, others see you. I do recognize and agree with the school of psychology that states, success does not always determine the amount of positive self-esteem one has. Consider the following very carefully:

Success, no matter how big or small,
does validate worthiness, which is the
entryway to greater positive self-esteem.

In this chapter I will develop the theory and value of self-help as the prime ingredient in increasing one's positive self-esteem. The theory of self-help contains two basic principles.

One: *Every individual has within themselves some way or ways in which they can excel.*

Two: *True self-esteem and personal satisfaction, including success, happiness and peace of mind, is always obtained through positive self-esteem.*

You need to understand this theory, the concept of self-help, in its fuller light. The first principle within the theory suggests that you are a unique human being. Within your physical and mental makeup, you are the guardian of one or more dynamic ideas, talents or abilities through which you can excel.

Everyone has talent. *That includes you.* Everyone can formulate ideas. *That includes you.* Ideas have consequences. Positive ideas produce positive results. When you apply the results to the best of your ability, excellence follows.

Some people have a lack of self-esteem because of their lack of education. A quality education is always of great benefit. However, throughout history many people have demonstrated that exceptional intellect and education have little to do with success.

The fact is, if you possess basic reading, writing and math skills, there is a place for you in the banquet hall of success. The second principle in this theory suggests that success and personal achievement is a matter of looking inside ourselves, independent of others for our self-worth and our success.

"But wait a minute," the professionals will cry. "People who have a negative or low self-esteem cannot look inside themselves, for when they do, they find pain, despair and negative attributes that they apply to themselves." I agree that many times this is the case. Nevertheless, my point is that it does not have to be.

As I have stated in a previous chapter, here is a fundamental law of success thinking:

"You can think only one thought at a time."

You cannot think about the negative at the same time as you are thinking about a positive. That is a success law of the universe.

In the next few pages, I will show you how to think of yourself as a winner, not a loser, as a success, not a failure. If you heed carefully, you will learn how to control the thoughts that flow through your mind. Then you will see yourself making the right choices. You will see yourself as someone of value and purpose.

There are seven key stages in the process of developing greater self-esteem.

Each of these stages are steps that overlap one another but each one has its own important value. In addition, each of these ideas begins in the mind and end in the mind. Here is the secret formula: First, there is the visualization process; your dreams and your goals. Visualization awakens your desire to be more successful.

The second step is to become a *doer*. You begin working to find ways that your dreams can come true. At this point, you do not have all the answers but you press forward. This daily *doing* is what develops in you, a certain know-how.

The third stage, you are now learning to be more effective. The fourth stage is experience. By visualizing, doing and developing know-how, you now have some success experiences upon which you can build.

The fifth stage is self-confidence. As a doer, you are constantly expanding and building on your know-how and experience. You are moving in the direction of your goal and your mind and spirit are beginning to throw off positive thoughts that create in you a greater self-confidence.

The sixth stage is the realization of self-worth. You now have discovered you are a person of worth and value. You are valuable first to your creator, to yourself, your family and to others. You have worth and more importantly you can see it, measure it and touch it.

The seventh and final stage is increased positive self-esteem. You feel better and better about yourself. Regardless of what you have or have not been told in the past, you are now becoming a new positive person. You are on your way to success and personal achievement, which can never really be attained without a strong, positive self-esteem. Write these words down; see how each stage represents a flow, a positive force coming out of you into the real world and back again to you.

Again, here are the seven key stages;

- *One: Visualization, which leads to two: Doing.*

- *Doing leads to three: Know-How.*

- *Know-How leads to four: Experience.*

- *Experience leads to five: Self-Confidence.*

- *Self-Confidence leads to six: Worthiness.*

- *Worthiness leads to seven: Increased Positive Self-esteem.*

Increased positive self-esteem leads to a happy, abundant, prosperous, successful life with peace of mind. I now want to further expand on each of these seven key stages and show you their full value, their usefulness and *coach you on their application in leading you to success.* If you master these seven stages, you will have discovered the reality of how success, real success, is achieved.

First: *Visualization*

The idea here is to dream a big dream, a dream that puts you in the winner's circle. Select goals for your life that when achieved will create a sense of personal accomplishment.

While visualizing your goals, it is important to not think about what you *do not have* and *cannot do*; only think about what *you do have and can do.* In addition, do not let the negative comments of others get you down on yourself.

Remember the words of Anna Eleanor Roosevelt:

"No one can make you feel inferior without your consent."

It is true. Just keep your eye on your dream; even if you do not know how, your dream will come true. Just keep on dreaming. Remember:

The mind completes the picture you put into it.

Second: *Doing*

Now you have a dream. It is time to develop a game plan for success. As the saying goes, plan your work and then work your plan. Now it is time to take action. Regardless of how small your first step is, just take it. Do not worry about the results.

Do a positive thing and positive results will follow. Sometimes change will not happen overnight. Sometimes change is a slow process but it will happen if you just get started. Doing makes it happen.

Third: *Know-How*

As you begin to take action toward your goal, you begin to develop greater know-how. Your mind and body will respond positively to this increased power that is starting to flow into your life.

Fourth: *Experience*

You gain strength and courage as your experiences gather momentum. You are now pursuing your dream. You are, in effect, a craftsman. The doing and know-how are creating valuable experiences in your life. You are beginning to understand the vast potential you have. You are now becoming a person with experience in your background. You will like this new you.

Fifth: *Self-Confidence*

Once you were fearful of the future but now those emotions are passing away. Self-confidence is the order of the day. You have lived in the bad times and now you are through them you can overcome any obstacle. You now do the very thing you used to think you could not do. You are transformed. Your confidence level is soaring.

Sixth: *Worthiness*

You are a doer. You have know-how, experience and self-confidence. These four great attributes are going to impact your life in a strong, positive way. As a result, you will be able to say to the real world you live in, "Hey world, look this way. Here is somebody who has value. I am a winner. I know where I am going and I know how to get there. Look out success; here I come."

Seventh: *Self-Esteem*

The other words, *visualization, doing, know-how, experience, self-confidence* and now *worthiness* all work together to create in you a greater awareness of who and what you are.

You now feel good about yourself. You are now mature enough to know that you and you alone have to make the decision to be a winner. You now realize that in the past you lived in self-limitation.

You now accept the responsibility to change that. You now face the world with a new, passionate desire to succeed.

Old thoughts and ways have been replaced by new thoughts and ways. Positive self-esteem now flows through your life. You have become a different person, a person with positive self-esteem.

I now have sixteen *Richer Life Secret* success principles to give you. These are gems of success coaching to help you in continuing to grow in greater positive self-esteem. Each of these sixteen secret success principles will work for you. How do I know that? They have already worked for countless others.

THE FIRST SECRET SUCCESS PRINCIPLE:

Practice Daily Seeing Yourself In Your Mind's Eye Exactly As You Would Like To Be Five Years From Now.

Where will you be living? What will your income be? What about your family life? What about your social life? How much will your vocabulary, education, talents and skills improve? Write a description of how you would like to be five years from now.

By doing this you begin the process of developing long-range goals. In time you will refine your goals, crystallizing them, challenging yourself to become the person you see in your mind. This is a great way to start to build your positive self-esteem. See yourself in a positive light. It is your choice.

People who have low self-esteem are people who have either no positive goals or they are constantly seeing the negative side of life, suggesting to them that they are not as good as other people, not as talented, not as smart. The list of negatives is unending.

By writing out a positive five-year lifestyle description, seeing your life exactly as you would like it to be five years from now, you begin the processes of preparing yourself for success. More importantly, you are taking control of your thinking.

You are becoming the master of your own fate, on course for personal growth and prosperity. This is the first step to exercising the axiom *to think is to create.*

When you study the lives of successful people, one attribute of success is present in each of them: they knew what they *wanted* out of their lives. They had written down these thoughts and made them a part of their daily mental and physical activities. Follow their example and you are on your way to a life filled with happiness and peace of mind: the *Richer Life.*

THE SECOND SECRET SUCCESS PRINCIPLE:
Establish And Affirm Aloud
A Positive Weekly Affirmation.

In previous chapters I have been over positive affirmations, their value and so forth. The point I want to make here is that positive affirmations, when meditated upon and shared with other positive people, will increase your positive self-esteem.

Therefore, write your positive weekly affirmation on a three-by-five card, meditate on it and read it aloud at least three times a day. Let yourself hear it early in the morning and late in the evening.

Do not let a single day go by without meditating on your positive affirmation. Begin seeing yourself becoming the person on your affirmation card.

Positive affirmations, repeated over and over, day and night, seven days a week, will, in time, not only increase your positive self-esteem; you will in fact, become the person of your affirmations. Once again, *the mind completes the picture you put into it.*

THE THIRD SECRET SUCCESS PRINCIPLE:
Foster A Spirit of Self-Kindness.

Growing up you were probably taught to be kind to others, especially to those less fortunate. Perhaps though, no one ever told you it is also wise to be kind to yourself. You will discover if you have not already, that you have flaws in your life. Hey, everyone does. It is just part of being human. In this light, why not be kinder to yourself?

Give yourself the right to be human.

I would never suggest someone do less than their best at anything, however part of maturing is simply realizing that you are not always going to be the best or number one in everything; no one is. So learn to be kind to yourself.

If you are like most people, you are far too harsh on yourself. It is right to challenge yourself, to push yourself to the limit. However, when you do not measure up to your expectations, give yourself a break. If you are not sure how to start this, just be as kind to yourself as you are to others.

Do not misunderstand. I am not suggesting that you make excuses for personal mistakes, being lazy or allowing yourself to slide when you know you could have done better.

What I am saying is that you will have those moments when you fail to do what should have been done. At these times, analyze the problem, learn from it, determine what needs to be done and do it. And be kind to yourself.

THE FOURTH SECRET SUCCESS PRINCIPLE:
Do Not Concern Yourself With What Others Are Doing. Keep Your Eye On What You Are Doing.

People are prone to judge themselves by what others around them are doing. For instance, people often think they are a failure because they

do not have the income their brother-in-law has or because they may not have the talent to do what a friend can do. Frankly speaking, there is not one plausible reason why you should judge yourself by another.

The real key to feeling good about yourself is not, *"Am I on par with others?"* Rather, positive self-esteem is built in your life when you pursue your own dream, achieving at a rate that suits your personality and ability.

You will always be able to find people who are better than you are at some things and others who are inferior to you. None of that matters. Judeo-Christian scriptures offer a keen insight on this topic. Consider this:

> *Each of us should test his own*
> *actions. Then he can take pride in*
> *himself without comparing himself to others.*

In other words, what really matters is whether you have set specific personal goals for your life, whether you are you committed to doing your best to achieve those goals. That is what counts. As soon as you have, you are then a person of purpose, value and promise.

THE FIFTH SECRET SUCCESS PRINCIPLE:
You Do Have An Infinite Right To Success.

While reading this book, I am sure this has become a familiar theme to you. At least I hope so. I cannot say it enough. You *do not* have to take a backseat to anyone. As a human being, you are the crowning achievement of all creation; you have been given the frame for success. It is up to you to clothe this frame your creator has given you, developing your own special individuality.

In accepting the fact that you do have an infinite right to success, do not expect to be empowered by anyone—not the government, your employer or some association. Everything you need for success, for real, positive individual success, has been given to you. Claim it today.

THE SIXTH SECRET SUCCESS PRINCIPLE:
Understand It Will Take Time.

Developing positive self-esteem is not an overnight package. You cannot rush to the front door and receive it. As in nearly everything great and valuable that comes your way, you can expect it to take some time. This is doubly true of increasing your positive self-esteem.

The key here is to fill up the vacuum of time with positive thoughts. You may want to write a letter to yourself relating the good things that have happened in your life or create a list of talents and abilities you know are part of your makeup. Use time wisely; set aside moments each day to visit with yourself.

This concept may be new to you but it is a valuable one. Since it takes time to change, help time along. Make the time of your life work for you. Remember, as I have said before:

Time is what we have;
wisdom is how we use it.

THE SEVENTH SECRET SUCCESS PRINCIPLE:
Practice Being The
Person of Your Dreams.

Think about this, all of your personal mannerisms and the dominating thoughts of your life were formed by habit and habit is developed by doing a specific thing in a specific way repeatedly. So the manners you wish to have, the thoughts, the outer actions of body, mind and spirit can be altered, changed or reinforced with practice. Take the quality of cheerfulness. If you practice being a person of good cheer, you will soon form it into a habit. It will in time, be something you do and not even think about. In fact, you will become known by your peers and coworkers as a cheerful person. Their inner thoughts about you will be altered by what they see and hear repeatedly.

In spite of what you may have heard, practice does not make perfect but practice does make permanent. And that is all you need.

THE EIGHTH SECRET SUCCESS PRINCIPLE:
Be Honest With Yourself.

One of the traits of people who do not have positive self-esteem is that they are seldom honest with themselves. They will deny their need for greater positive self-esteem, hiding away their true feelings about themselves.

The person who has a big ego is also often less than candid, hiding their true feelings about themselves, acting from an egotistical base, hoping to throw people off from seeing inside them and seeing that they are different from how they appear.

If you need greater positive self-esteem, that is not a crime. It is no sin. Everyone who is honest would confess they could do with a bit more of this marvelous quality. So be honest with yourself. Measure the positive self-esteem you have.

If you need more, apply these secret success principles to your life. Face it; if many people did not need added positive self-esteem, I would not be writing and coaching people about it now.

THE NINTH SECRET SUCCESS PRINCIPLE:
Be Open To New Ideas.

I once heard an associate of mine say there were only three tests to intelligence. If you could answer yes to three questions, you were a very intelligent person. Here are the three questions.

One: ***Can you entertain yourself?***

Two: ***Can you entertain others?***

Three: ***Can you entertain a new idea?***

How did you answer the three questions? Can you do those three things? If so, you are a person of intellect to be sure and just as importantly, you are a person who possesses positive self-esteem.

THE TENTH SECRET SUCCESS PRINCIPLE:
Be Open To Change.

This is a little like being open to new ideas, except you are going a step beyond and saying to yourself, *"If I need to make changes in my life, I will do it.*

I realize that whatever steps have to be taken, if they lead to greater positive self-esteem, it will be worth it." As you change, you will experience a deep feeling of greater self-worth.

That is your payoff. Your greater sense of self-worth will be reflected in your completely new life and that is called positive self-esteem.

THE ELEVENTH SECRET SUCCESS PRINCIPLE:
Self-Esteem Is Not Regulated By Outward Circumstance But By Inner Thought.

Circumstances of all sorts fall to everyone. Yes, it is true that some circumstances are predetermined by one's behavior however many circumstances just arrive at your doorstep.

You may feel very strongly the circumstance is not deserved and obviously, the circumstance is not wanted. Yet the circumstance is here and you have to deal with it.

While many people seem to think that this or that circumstance has caused them to have low self-esteem and perhaps contributed to their failure, in truth it is their reaction to circumstance, not the circumstance itself, that raises or lowers their self-esteem.

Their thoughts will determine their reaction and remember you can always control your thoughts. As you already discovered, you can think only one thought at a time, so choose a good, positive thought. This will bring about a positive reaction to the circumstance.

THE TWELFTH SECRET SUCCESS PRINCIPLE:

More Often Than Not, People Fail
Not From A Lack Of Talent Or Knowledge,
But From A Lack Of Perspective.

There are literally millions of men and women in each generation who have talent and knowledge in abundance but their lives are in shambles. The undercurrent of poor self-esteem has lowered their vision and they cannot see even the horizon of perspective, let alone through the kaleidoscope of vision.

Perspective, image and *vision*: These valuable tools of the trade produce successful people. With perspective, a vista view dominates your thinking. You are not bound by circumstance, mistakes or how other people think.

You possess the ability to see afar and to act upon that inner sight. With a *visionary perspective*, your mind thinks the best, hopes the best, feels the best and ultimately enjoys the best.

THE THIRTEENTH SECRET SUCCESS PRINCIPLE:

Accept The Fact That You Will Make
Some Mistakes As You Pursue Your Goals.

Mistakes are unavoidable if you are to achieve success. You cannot expect to be perfect at every turn. Achieving success is a series of twists and turns on the road of life. To be jolted and detoured on occasion is par for the course. Too many people, *I trust you are not numbered among them,* think their world is coming apart just because they made a mistake or two. There are three positive things about making mistakes. Consider each of them carefully.

One: ***Mistakes are a sign you tried something.***

While it is true in the business world, there is no payoff for trying; you are paid only for doing. Trying, even if you do not succeed, often produces the answers to questions that eventually lead to achievement and success. Moreover, very often *great success* follows on the heels of *great mistakes*.

Two: **Mistakes can be a great teacher.**

I can tell you a little-known truth: generally speaking, *you learn more from your mistakes than your victories*. Why? Usually you remember your mistakes longer. They stick in your craw and they drive you to redeem yourself.

Three: **Mistakes can be a valuable learning experience.**

There is no on-the-job training for life-success as there is for a host of other skills or opportunities. Success is that elusive quality of life that you either achieve or not. Mistakes, though they may seem burdensome for the moment, can actually be valuable learning experiences leading you to a new awareness, understanding and direction for success.

> ## THE FOURTEENTH SECRET SUCCESS PRINCIPLE:
> ### You Can Fail And Still Succeed.

Setbacks, even failure, are all part of becoming a success. Take, for example, Major League Baseball players and the subject of hitting. Even the very best fail to get on base 60 to 70 percent of the time. Think of it. They fail 60 to 70 percent of the time.

At times life can be like that. In the struggle for success, you will have some bad days, weeks, months or even years. That is life. Yet there is one thing you need to understand: *failure is never final.* It is true. Failure is never final.

**There will always be an opportunity
coming along immediately after any failure.**

Life does not stop with the setbacks. Even bankruptcy does not halt your opportunity to succeed. Everything that has happened to you I guarantee has happened to others. Yes, life gobbles some people up but not you.

You have vision, specific goals and a plan of action. You will achieve the victory. You will win because now, you know deep down inside that is your destiny.

THE FIFTEENTH SECRET SUCCESS PRINCIPLE:
Remember The 80/20 Rule.

Vilfredo Pareto was an economist who is credited with establishing what is now widely known as the Pareto Principle or 80/20 rule. When he discovered the principle, it established that 80% of the land in Italy was owned by 20% of the population.

Later, he discovered that the Pareto principle was valid in other parts of his life, such as gardening: 80% of his garden peas were produced by 20% of the peapods. The assumption is that a small number of causes determine most of the results in any situation.

80/20 Thinking, applied to your daily personal and business life, can help you change behavior and to concentrate on the most important 20%. Action resulting from 80/20 thinking should lead you to achieve much more with much less.

To engage in 80/20 thinking, you must constantly ask yourself, what is the 20% that is leading to 80%? Never assume that you automatically know what the answer is, take time to think creatively about it. The key theme of the 80/20 Principle applied to your life and business is how to create the greatest value and generate the most profits with the least expenditure of assets and efforts. The 80/20 rule always creates opportunities for genuine entrepreneurs and innovators.

THE SIXTEENTH SECRET SUCCESS PRINCIPLE:

Hold Onto Your Dream; Never Give Up On Your Dream.

When setbacks occur and slow going seems to engulf you, remember this: *you can turn it around*. Just keep on keeping on. Stay in the game. *Do not give up*. You may have to regroup. So be it.

You may have to create a totally new game plan. If that is what it takes, do it. There is a beautiful, successful person inside of you just waiting to get out. Stand where you are. Do not give up any more ground. Life will yield to you its best. No matter what happens, just keep dreaming your dream. Just keep on keeping on!

Now you have the sixteen life-changing secret success principles. These are tools upon which to build your life. These success principles will enhance your positive self-esteem.

Remember, success is your destiny. The quicker you act like it, look like it, feel like it, the sooner it will happen.

You now have another *Richer Life Secret* that will lead you to the life of your dreams. Your feelings about yourself, no matter how positive, can never plumb the depths of your true potential. Your potential for success is limitless.

This universe is designed so that it can create for you any dream you envision, no matter how large. Today is your day. Apply these sixteen secret success principles to your life and you will be living the *Richer Life*!

*You Are Never Bigger Than
The Problem That Stops You.*

Rick C. Ernst

CHAPTER THIRTEEN

SUCCESSFUL PROBLEM SOLVING AND DECISION MAKING

I want to stress at the outset of this chapter that what I am about to relate to you regarding the subject of problem solving and decision making is very important. It is safe to say that the twin setbacks of not solving the problems one faces and of not making the right decisions, have stopped more men and women from becoming successful than any other deficiencies in their lives. You will want to study this chapter carefully, for what you are about to learn is literally life changing.

Consider the word *problem* for just a moment. Just saying this word often raises the hair on the back of ones neck. Some immediately begin to tense up. Therefore a better and more positive understanding of what a problem is needs to be brought out into the open. Here are four concepts that will put the view of the word problem in a new and positive light.

One: *A problem is an unsolved opportunity.*

That is really an apt description of a problem. When you solve any problem, you will invariably find one or more opportunities. You will quickly discover as you watch highly successful people at work that they almost seem to delight when a problem arises, because they know the problem that confronts them is really an opportunity in disguise.

Two: *A problem is never as large or threatening as when it is first expressed.*

In the first instance, when most people perceive they have a problem or a potential problem, a sort of panic sets in. Worry becomes the order of the moment. Why? They have set their eyes on the problem instead of on the possible opportunities and solutions.

In his book *The Art of Selfishness* David Seabury strikes this analogy; In South Africa miners dig for diamonds. They are willing to lift tons of earth to find a little pebble not as large as your little fingernail. People often forget this principle and become pessimists because there is more dirt than diamonds.

When problems come, do not be frightened by the negatives. Look for the positives. And dig them out! The more you look at a problem, the more you will see that it is never as large and threatening as it first appeared.

In fact, if you stay positive and focused, a solution circumstance will yield to you several exciting and profitable ideas. So keep digging; the problem will turn into an opportunity.

Three: *Every adversity carries with it a seed of an equal or greater benefit.*

This most basic of all axioms concerning problems has been a unique part of successful people's lives. These people find the seeds of opportunities in both their problems and their blessings. Why? Because they look for them, they are determined to *accentuate the positive, eliminate the negative.* You use your positive attitude to see deep inside the problem that confronts you. As you do, the seeds of equal or greater benefit are born. As they grow you swiftly move from the point of having a problem to actually benefiting from the problem.

Four: *A roadblock or a detour is never final; it is simply an irritation or delay.*

This is how problems need to be seen. All roadblocks are finally removed and all detours are finally repaired. A problem may delay you for a day, a week, a month or sometimes longer but eventually you will be back on your way to success. No problem can stop the person who will not settle for less than the best.

I now turn your attention to ten steps for solving problems. You will discover that many of the solutions offered in this ten-step program have more to do with your attitude than with anything else. The reason is, as has been said, your attitude determines your altitude. Here then, are the ten tried and true solutions I use and so can you.

THE FIRST STEP FOR SOLVING A PROBLEM:
A Problem Well Stated Is A Problem Half Solved.

This is an old proverb but it also states a great truth. When you encounter a problem, before you go off in forty different directions, take the time to *analyze* it. Look at it from all sides until you can answer this simple question: *what is the problem?* Put it into a simple statement you can write on a piece of paper. Then reduce it to its lowest common denominator. Once you can see the problem for what it is, it will be far easier to start the solution process. Do not hurry yourself. Act out of wisdom, not out of panic. Have the courage to lay the problem aside until you feel you are mentally and emotionally prepared to deal with it.

THE SECOND STEP FOR SOLVING A PROBLEM:
Accept The Fact That Problems Are Reality.

Over the years I have known many people who refuse to accept that problems of life are real. It is the mentality that says, "If I refuse to acknowledge the problem as real, it will go away." Believe me. It does not work that way. Problems are real. No matter how hard you try, you cannot run from your problems. They have a way of following you. You can be like an ostrich and stick your head in the sand. You can even deny a problem exists. However, reality is reality and if you refuse to face it, many times your problem will simply loom larger and larger until you cannot possibly succeed.

THE THIRD STEP FOR SOLVING A PROBLEM:
You Are No Bigger Than The Problem That Stops You.

Throughout time, millions of men and women so close to success have allowed a problem to stop their forward progress. Just a little more effort and all their dreams would have come true; so close and yet so far away. Here are two life-changing axioms. If you make these two concepts a part of your life, living with them every day, no problem will ever stop you.

One: *Hold your ground even when you would rather run.*

Problems are solved, most of the time, by slowly but surely inching your way upward and over the problem to success. But hear this well: there will be many days when you would like to run as far away as you possibly can. Yet you hold your ground. You refuse to back down. You bow your back. You move as far forward as you can. How? Just one-step at a time.

Two: *In trying times, work hard even when every fiber of your being says quit.*

I heard a story about a small boy who was having a confrontation with his mother over a recently purchased pair of Rollerblades. The boy was bleeding from cut knees and hands from falling on the concrete. His mother lovingly said, "Johnny, why don't you give up?" He said, "Mom, I didn't get these Rollerblades to quit with; I got them to learn with."

I can promise you in your success journey, there will be many days when you will be ready to give it all up. You will say to yourself, "I can't go another step." Yes, you can. Why? You can always take just one more step. The key is to keep your eye on the goal. Then push yourself; push yourself again and again, one step at a time. Just take one step after another. That is the key.

Once again, it is important you have this third step clear in your mind: *You are never bigger than the problem that stops you.*

When the road gets rough, here is a thought that drives me. It is a challenge to my inner being to think that if I quit now, I will be known as a person who was stopped by this or that problem. Anything that gets in your way should be seen as a serious enemy to your dreams of success and prosperity.

Negativity clothes itself in a myriad of small and large problems. You must constantly be on your guard, ready and anxious to defeat any situation that confronts you. The struggle between the negative and the positive must be seen for what it is: *warfare.* Your frame of mind must be that you will soundly defeat anything that stands in your way and that you will take no prisoners.

THE FOURTH STEP FOR SOLVING A PROBLEM:
Avoid Worry.

It is a proven fact. Worry has already killed more people than work. The reason that worrying has killed more people than work is that more people worry than work. All of us worry to varying degrees. However, we were not born that way. Worrying is a learned process. So if you have learned to worry, you can learn not to worry. I know many people who think they are actually being very responsible when they worry, not realizing that each moment of worry is a waste of time and energy that steals the joy and satisfaction they should get from their work and life.

There are four basic ways in which people fall into the worry habit.

There may be countless others but these four seem to show up constantly on the surveys asking people what they worry about.

One: **Worrying over the unknown.**

Sometimes you are in a situation where you know something has to be done but you are not sure what. So you begin to worry. I challenge you; instead of worrying, develop a list of options. This is, as Robert Schuller would say, *"possibility thinking."* When you have your *option list* made, think and study. Choose what you believe to be the best option and act. Believe me, that sure beats sitting around worrying.

Two: **Worrying over the future.**

You have a big decision coming up. You cannot do anything at this very moment but think about it. Do not worry. Put the future in its proper place: *in the future.* You can begin to prepare for this future decision in a number of ways.

You can write down the exact date you will make the decision. You can begin to gather facts and information, creating the options. Then, every time the worry returns, simply remind yourself: *I am on target. It is being handled.* Give yourself the credit you deserve.

Three: **Worrying over the events of the past.**

Read these next sentences slowly and carefully.

The past does live in you, but you do not have to live in the past.

You can of course, learn from the past but to live in regret with the *could haves* and *should haves* is an exercise in futility. The past is just that, passed and you cannot change it.

Four: ***Worrying over procrastination.***

When you have a problem and need to take action and fail to do so, your mental and emotional system will find it almost *natural* to worry. If you have learned to procrastinate, then you can also learn to take the responsibility for each day's effort. If you have a deadline, meet it. Take charge.

Worrying about *the past*; *the unknown*; *the future*; and *procrastination*, will not get you where you want to be." You learned to worry and with a little practice, you can learn to stamp out worry by taking positive action. One last thought about worry. If you just have to keep dwelling on your problem, why not do so in prayer? For it was the great disciple Peter who, in 1 Peter 5:7, said: *"Cast your anxieties on him, for he cares for you."*

THE FIFTH STEP FOR SOLVING A PROBLEM:
Accept The Problem Or Situation For What It Is; Do Not Pretend.

As I pointed out in Step Four, worrying is never a good idea but neither is pretending that everything is okay when it is not. In pretending, you are not dealing with the problem, you are only pushing forward the problem. No matter how painful, learn to face the facts. The rule is simple, if you have a problem, face it.

THE SIXTH STEP FOR SOLVING A PROBLEM:
Do Not Dwell On What Went Wrong; Focus On What To Do Next.

Human nature being what it is, whenever a problem arises, if you are not careful, you will spend most of your time thinking about what went wrong. If personalities are involved, you may even begin to place blame and before you know it, you are completely bogged down. If you lose your focus by taking your eyes off your goal, your problem will compound itself.

When a problem presents itself, begin immediately to make a list of the things that can be done to solve the problem as quickly as possible. There will be ample time for reflection later. As you focus on ways and means to solve the problem, take notes; or better yet, keep a running diary of the situation. After things are back to normal, your notes will often provide good ideas to keep this particular problem from ever happening again.

THE SEVENTH STEP FOR SOLVING A PROBLEM:
Be Careful In Selecting Experts To Help You In Solving A Problem.

It has been my experience that so-called experts know all the reasons you cannot do something. Seldom do experts come armed with a bag of solutions. It is not their nature to go out on a limb and tell you what you should do.

Do not misunderstand; I am not against wise counsel. As a matter of fact, Proverbs 15:22 encourages one to always get wise counsel.

I am against the so-called experts that earn their living slowing you down or telling you all the ways something will not work. Wise counsel, on the other hand, is looking for all the ways something will work for you in the decision-making process.

These people will help you keep moving forward in a positive manner always looking for the best solution. In addition, wise counsel is not afraid to challenge your ideas but if and when they do, it is because they have an idea they think will better solve your problem.

THE EIGHTH STEP FOR SOLVING A PROBLEM:
Always Ask Direct Questions.

This eighth step has its best application when you are in a staff or group setting but it also works when you are alone. For sure, there will be a different list of questions for each problem you face, yet some standard questions will always be in order. Among those will be:

- *What exactly is the problem?*

- *When did it first begin to manifest itself?*

- *Who is involved?*

- *What can we do to stop the problem?*

- *What can we do in the future so that this problem never occurs again?*

These are good questions because they are direct questions. They cut through the hemming and hawing that often occurs when a problem arises. You want to get to the heart of the problem as fast as you can. The sooner the better—while all of the ramifications of the problem are clear in your mind.

THE NINTH STEP FOR SOLVING A PROBLEM:
No Problem Is So Difficult That The Solution Cannot Be Discovered By Seeking A Truthful Answer.

This ninth step assumes you are going to make an honest effort to get to the heart of the problem and solve it no matter how painful it might be. If you are serious about getting the answer out in the open, you can do it. Sometimes we know almost immediately what the problem is and how to solve it but it still may be painful, embarrassing or costly. So we just postpone the whole affair. Guess what? A problem does not just sit there where you left it.

Problems seem to take on lives of their own. Someone no stranger to the *Richer Life Secrets* gave us a greater insight into the solution of problems when he said:

> *"Ask and you shall receive;*
> *seek and you shall find;*
> *knock and the door will be opened."*

The master teacher, Jesus, is right. *Ask, seek, knock* and you will discover the truth of the matter. In addition, you will also be given positive ideas that you can use to solve the problem and get yourself focused again; where success and personal achievement will be awarded to you.

THE TENTH STEP FOR SOLVING A PROBLEM:
Stay Positive About The Future.

Robert Schuller was right on when he said:

> *"Failure is never final."*

Sometimes it seems you are in a problem so deep it will be impossible to turn your life around. I know I have been there and so have a million other successful people. The key:

> *No matter how desperate*
> *your immediate situation is,*
> *stay positive about the future.*

It was Edmund Burke, the great English statesman, who wrote,

> *"You can never plan your future by your past."*

He is right. Each new day brings with it twenty-four hours of explosive, life-changing opportunity. Today a problem has you pinned to the ground. Tomorrow you plant the seeds of this problem's benefits deep into the soil of your subconscious and, in a very short time, you will rebound and move forward toward the completion of your goals.

Remember, the present or the past is never an indication of your future. You have today this moment. In addition, problems always look less threatening in a new day's light. So stay positive. You will climb to the top.

Let us review for just a moment, reflecting on the ten great ideas you now have for solving the problems that come your way as you work toward the completion of your goals.

1. A problem well stated is half solved.

2. Problems are reality.

3. You are no bigger than the problem that stops you.

4. Avoid worry.

5. Accept the problem for what it is; do not pretend.

6. Do not dwell on what went wrong; focus on what to do next.

7. Be careful in selecting experts to help you in solving a problem.

8. Ask direct questions.

9. No problem is so difficult that the solution cannot be discovered by seeking a truthful answer.

10. Stay positive about the future.

As you apply these ten problem-solving techniques to your life and work, you will have taken a giant step forward toward full and lasting success. Let us turn now to the second consideration of this chapter, that of making decisions.

It goes without saying that problems are ultimately solved only when wise decisions are made. Therefore, in addition to the ten steps to solving the problems that arise in your life;

There are six effective key principles to a successful decision-making process.

As you master these sixteen dynamic ideas, the ten problem-solving techniques and the six wise decision-making concepts, one thing is for sure you will be taking charge of the present and future years of your life.

The first key principle of making a wise decision:

Demonstrate your courage; do something.

When I was growing up, my father used to say, "Do something even if it's wrong." That sounds like negative advice but it is not. Sometimes a decision must be made and you are not always in a position to know exactly what to do. In these times, you must have the courage to begin. Take action. Something good will ultimately come from it. As I said, there will be times when you do not know exactly what to do but you must make a decision. However, when I reach that point I always make sure I have prayed about the decision before me.

The second key principle of making a wise decision:

Understand the positive value of pressure.

When it comes time to make an important decision it seems there is always pressure but in my view that is good. Your mental and emotional systems come alive; thoughts fly out of your brain at a faster and faster rate. You are now completely focused. Good ideas will surface. Pressure can be a very healthy thing, a valuable thing. Think of a piece of coal. When it is put under intense pressure it becomes a precious stone, a diamond. So it is with you. You can turn pressure into success.

The third key principle of making a wise decision:

Decisions offer new opportunities
for a positive change.

Any time you make a decision, it is as if you throw a rock into a pond. The ripples immediately begin to expand and ultimately push themselves across the pond to the other shore.

A positive decision will send ripples through out the lake of your life. Decisions stir things up. Decisions cause you look at life differently.

This action creates new opportunities for personal growth, expand and succeed.

The fourth key principle of making a wise decision:

More is lost by indecision
than by wrong decision.

If you take the time to research success and failure in the lives of others and in your own life, you will discover this salient point:

People rarely fail because
they make a wrong decision;
People fail because they delay
or refuse to make a decision.

You see, if you make a decision, even a wrong decision, you have acted. You have set in motion a returning flood of circumstance. If you have made a wrong decision, once you discover it, make it right and keep moving forward toward your goal of success and prosperity.

If you make no decision at all, it is as if life has stopped for you and to be perfectly frank, it has. There are times when trying to make a good decision can be terrifying but to make no decision at all is the ultimate bad decision.

The fifth key principle of making a wise decision:

Do not worry about making a right decision;
make a decision and make it right.

I like this concept. It is also a great truth. In decision making, many times you are not sure the decision you make is the best one, the right one. However, I have discovered in my life that if after making a decision, I do everything in my power to make this decision work, it usually does.

One thing to avoid at all times is simply making a decision and then just sitting back to see what will happen. Throw yourself into your own life. Do not wait for circumstance or for others to decide what is best for you. Take charge. Get in control. Research, study, seek the best coaching and of course, pray. Do everything you can to make all the decisions of your life the right ones, the very best you can make.

The sixth key principle of making a wise decision:

When making financial decisions apply the three golden rules of finance.

The first rule is a basic proverb that is 3,500 years old and one I have already introduced to you in a previous chapter but it is so important I want to share it again:

The borrower is servant to the lender.

When you take on a debt, you take on additional responsibility. First you have the responsibility to repay the loan. In addition, there is usually interest on the loan. In this light, loans of money, no matter how easy they are to come by, may not be in your best interest.

The second golden rule of finance:

Price is an invitation to purchase, not a factual statement as to real value.

Almost everything sold has at least three prices:

One, the manufacturer's price to the wholesaler.

Two, the wholesaler's price to the retailer.

Three, the retailer's price to you.

The secret to remember is:

To find the best price, it is always where and when you buy.

The third golden rule of finance:

Terms are often more important than price.

There are times when who you pay, how you pay and when you pay are more important than what you pay.

Here is an example: As a real estate investor, I located a home that I knew I could purchase and resell in a short time. So I agreed to the price and the very high interest rate.

All this was agreed to in order to put the house under contract with a very small down payment and lengthen out the closing date to 160 days instead of the usual period of time. Sure enough, in less than ninety days I sold the house for a very good profit.

The key to this profitable venture was the great terms I had worked out. So remember, price is not always the major consideration.

Here is a review of these six key principles of decision making:

1. Demonstrate your courage and act.

2. Understand the positive value of pressure.

3. Decisions offer new opportunities for a positive change.

4. More is lost by indecision than by wrong decision.

5. Do not worry about making a right decision. Make a decision; then make it right.

6. When making financial decisions, apply the three golden rules of finance.

With these six key principles of decision making, together with the ten key steps of problem solving, you now have another sixteen *Richer Life Secrets*. These success principles will help you take charge of any and every circumstance of life.

Throughout history, effective problem solvers and decision makers have influenced the destinies of millions of people. They are in fact, the movers and shakers in every generation.

Now that you have these sixteen secret key principles in your life, you are destined for success. No problem will stop you. No decision will frighten you. You are the captain of your own ship of prosperity. So set sail; you are assured favorable winds!

CHAPTER
FOURTEEN

NEGOTIATING YOUR WAY TO SUCCESS

L et me ask you a question, are you a negotiator? It is safe to say that every human being is a negotiator. Perhaps you have not thought of yourself in this light. Follow this conversation that takes place thousands of times each day.

"Honey," says the husband, "I'm going to be late tonight. I have a meeting after work with the vice president. Could you swing by the cleaners before they close and pick up my shirts?" "Okay," responds the wife. "However, I need you to stop by the store on your way home and pick up a few things. The list is on the table in the hallway. Could you do that for me?" "Alright," says the husband.

This is an example of successful negotiation that takes place in a family setting. Both parties had a specific need that they were able to verbalize in a clear and forthright manner and both parties were able to get what was important to them. That, in a micro view, is what all negotiation is.

Within this chapter, I will share with you nine concepts and seven key proven and effective concepts in the art of negotiation.

The first concept: Defining the term, *negotiating your way to success*.

Every person negotiates every day. Some negotiations are as simple as the above illustration I just gave you of the husband and wife. Other negotiations can be more difficult, especially if one party is against or negative toward the negotiator.

In addition, negotiations can often be long and difficult when you are negotiating various forms of contracts. Webster's dictionary says *to negotiate is to clear, to vault, to surmount, to leap.* That is exactly what a successful negotiation does. It clears away the problem so that both people or groups can see each other's viewpoints.

It vaults over disagreements to find a common ground. It surmounts obstacles because a proper negotiating spirit creates a positive atmosphere. Finally, it leaps to a clear accounting of all the facts from which definitive answers will be forthcoming, resulting in a mutual agreement in the best interest of all concerned.

In any field of knowledge or expertise, there is what is called the *fundamentals* or the *basics* and the basics must not only be mastered but they must always be in view.

I am sure you have heard at least one football coach say, "The reason we lost the game is we forgot the basics. We did not block, tackle, run, pass or punt like we had been taught. We left the basics in the locker room."

To make sure that does not happen to you, I have singled out the following nine basic steps to becoming a successful negotiator. These steps will give you a decided edge in working out large or small negotiations.

Number one: ***In a successful negotiation, both sides win.***

Negotiating is one of those rare races for the winner's circle in which both you and your opponent can be declared a winner. That is the object of negotiation.

However, your opponents may not be at all interested in your receiving what you want from the negotiation; they may only be interested in what they want. No matter, if you use these basic negotiating techniques I present in this chapter, both sides can and will win.

Number two: ***For a successful negotiation enter the negotiation with a good, pleasant countenance and smile.***

Just because you disagree with someone on an issue in a negotiation, that is no reason to be downcast, negative, sour or angered. In fact, holding onto a divisive spirit will work against you, prolong the argument, harden the opposition's point of view and risk the entire opportunity to settle the issue in your favor.

It does not cost you one thin dime to be pleasant. Smile as often as possible. Show your willingness to give and take. Demonstrate your earnest desire to settle the issue with both sides winning if possible. I can tell you this firsthand; during negotiating, *smiling is a powerful tool.*

Obviously, you cannot just sit there smiling the whole time. However, remember this simple rule:

> ***Make sure you are smiling***
> ***more than the one with***
> ***whom you are negotiating.***

Number three: ***For a successful negotiation be gracious, even when you do not feel like it.***

It may be that your opponent has spoken against your character, questioned your integrity or in other ways made it hard for you to be gracious but do it anyway. No matter how you feel, continue to be gracious.

The key to all negotiation is flexibility of spirit. Believe me you can break down the negative defenses of your opponent just as often through simply exhibiting a gracious manner as through a defensive discourse. This has worked for me many times and it will work for you too.

Number four: *For a successful negotiation see the world as your opponent views it.*

Every person has what can be called a worldview. A worldview is how you see things. In politics it may be a Democratic, Republican or Independent view. In economics it may be liberal or conservative. In religion it may be Catholic or Protestant.

In order to see why your opponents feel as they do, it is helpful to see the world from their point of view. As you discover more and more about their mindset, their worldview, you will see why they negotiate as they do. Then you can understand more fully why certain ideas and concepts may be more important to them than others.

Number five: *For a successful negotiation avoid legal arbitration if possible.*

Always try to keep the negotiating directly between the parties involved. Do everything you can to keep it from the legal profession. Why? Not all, mind you but far too many lawyers are *adversarial for profit only.* The longer they can keep two parties fighting, the longer they continue to make money, no matter which side eventually wins.

However, if the problem being negotiated is over your head, that is, you are not sure of all your legal rights or obligations, then by all means, consult a lawyer who best represents your worldview, your positive spirit, your willingness to be fair.

Number six: *For a successful negotiation always focus on the problem being negotiated not on the individuals involved.*

Over the years as I have counseled both married couples and coached businesses owners, in watching people argue, I have often discovered that as soon as the name-calling begins, any hope of solving the problem is out the window.

If you are to be successful in negotiating an agreement, no matter what the problem may be, you must not be guilty of name-calling and the castigation of the individuals on the other side.

No one falls lower down the scale of immaturity as when he stoops to attempt to win a point by trying to ruin the reputation of a fellow human being. It may be that the other side, your opponent, will be hostile or full of anger but you do not have to respond in like manner.

In fact, you can often win the day by staying calm, cool and collected exercising kindness with your emotions in check. Yes, at times it is hard but I have done it a thousand times and most of the time I got what I wanted in the negotiation. So can you.

A French proverb states:

What wisdom can you find that is greater than kindness?

Kindness is almost the perfect irresistible emotion. Some people are so eaten up with self-pity and hatred they are blinded to the reality that you care for them and want the best for them. Nevertheless, usually a demonstration of kindness is of great value to you during negotiation.

Aesop, in his famous fable, "The Lion and the Mouse," says, "No act of kindness, no matter how small, is ever wasted." He hit the nail dead center. Kindness is an emotion like love. Both flow from heart to heart. Words flow from head to head. Kindness enters the other person's heart. It softens. Its appeal to reason is gentle. This I know for sure:

There is a great power that comes from a gentle act of kindness.

Number seven: *For a successful negotiation attempt to serve, to give, to go the extra mile.*

In Judeo-Christian literature, we learn that *the creator loves a cheerful giver*. That is the application of this point. The object here is to prioritize your list of what you want from the negotiation. After making your list, number your wants in a priority system. Ask yourself, what is the most important thing I want? If I get that, what is the second, third and so on? Now you are ready to answer the question, where in this negotiation can I demonstrate my willingness to be a giver, to go the extra mile, to serve?

In addition, if it is possible, try to uncover the number one priority of your opponent. What do they really want? Once you get this out in the open, you are more clearly able to see what you can give away, proving your desire to get a settlement that your opponent agrees upon.

Number eight: ***For a successful negotiation whenever possible, keep everything simple.***

While there are hundreds of books written on negotiation, what most of this literature tends to do is muddy the water. What you want to do is keep things simple.

There are three elements to any negotiation:

One: **You**

Two: **Your opponent**

Three: **The problem**

That is it. There is never more or less. Keeping things simple means know what you want, know what your opponent wants and know what the real problem is. Concentrate on these three things. Everything else is minor.

Number nine: ***For a successful negotiation remember, while negotiating is often stressful, stress is not caused by the problem but by your reaction to it.***

When a problem occurs between two or more people, almost everyone's first reaction is emotional rather than factual. When we combine our emotions with the emotions of our opponents, soon a situation can become very stressful.

However, if you wish to become a wise, successful negotiator, always check your emotions by asking yourself *what are the facts*? Then immediately begin to put together a plan to solve the problem. Working on your plan will force you to act upon the *facts* rather than to stir up negative emotions that will be a hindrance to you.

Remember this:

Stress always comes from the emotional side of your being.

The facts and your success plan of action flow from the reasoning side of your being. This is the area to which a successful negotiator will commit himself. Do not worry about what others are saying or doing. Just calmly go about the business of building your case. Success will follow.

In summary, you can assuredly state you now know the basic steps of being a successful negotiator. I want to be sure you have them before we go on, so here is a brief review of the nine keys concepts of negotiating.

One: A successful negotiation has occurred when both sides get what they want.

Two: Enter the fray with a pleasant countenance and put on your best smile.

Three: Be gracious to your opponent even when you do not feel like it.

Four: See the world as your opponent views it.

Five: Avoid legal arbitration if possible.

Six: Always focus on the problem being negotiated, not on the individuals involved.

Seven: Attempt to be a servant, a giver; go the extra mile.

Eight: Keep everything simple.

Nine: Stress is not caused by the problem but by your reaction to it.

You must have a working knowledge of these basics keys of negotiating. Often, simply because you know how to use these negotiating skills, the problem will be settled swiftly, surely and to everyone's complete satisfaction.

There will be times, however, when you must move on past the *basics* and in earnest, with complete candor, fight it out on the battle-ground of negotiation. When this happens, these next seven principles will serve you well.

These principles are a proven winning formula. They are in fact, this chapter's secrets to negotiating your way to success.

THE FIRST SECRET PRINCIPLE:

Know Yourself.
Know Your Opponent.
Know The Situation Or Problem
You Are Trying To Negotiate.

There are three components in this first principle: Let us take a closer look at all three.

First: *It is important that you know yourself.*

That may sounds strange. *Know myself.* You may say you do know yourself. I am sure you do or at least you think you do. Let me ask you, "How will you act if your opponent tells a lie in an attempt to gain the high ground?"

Do you know yourself? How will you act if your opponent says disparaging things about you? Do you know yourself? At some point during a negotiation, you may become involved in a very intense and negative situation.

Do you know yourself? You cannot trust or expect for that matter—your opponent to be kind and considerate. In these times, do you know yourself?

What you need to be aware of is not the surprises that can occur or the obnoxious manner of your opponent but what your reaction could be. You want to be sure that you will be calm, cool, collected, in control of yourself at all times.

Second: *Know your opponent.*

At the top of the list of what you want to know about your opponent is why: why have they taken this arbitrary position? Why have they chosen to put you in a position where you run the risk of being made to be something you are not? What is your opponent's motivation? Find that out and you are more than halfway down the road to completing the negotiation.

Like many others, life has taught me some things books never could. For instance, a person often has two reasons for what he does the reason he gives you and the *real* reason he has hidden away.

Determining the other person's true motivation will not always be easy but it can be done. Sometimes the answer will come through observation or from people, who know your opponent, maybe from remarks your opponent has made or perhaps from something you learn about your opponent while doing in-depth research in preparation for the negotiation session.

Above all, in knowing your opponents, never underestimate them. I have watched top negotiators be taken for everything but their socks time after time, all because they underestimated their opponent's ability and motivation to win. So never underestimate your opponent.

Third: *Know the situation or problem you are trying to negotiate.*

One of the most common mistakes many people make in negotiation is to assume they know what the problem is. They make an educated guess rather than taking the necessary effort to really analyze the problem, to see the inner truths that will not be revealed by guesswork.

So again I say, know yourself, know your opponent and know the problem. In a nutshell, do your homework. It will be worth its weight in gold when the negotiating phase begins.

I always try to have two or three times the amount of information I will ever need or use during the negotiation. As the saying goes, *information is power.*

THE SECOND SECRET PRINCIPLE:
Decide Exactly What
You Want From The Negotiation.

Whatever else you may not be clear on, know this for sure, you never begin a negotiation with anyone until you are 100 percent sure *you know what you want.* This is your bottom line. It is your fallback position from which you will not retreat.

You may have compiled a rather large list of wishes, wants and maybes but in that list is the one thing or set of things that you have made up your mind that cannot and will not be negotiated away.

This focus is of utmost importance. Deciding what you want is not always easy. Here are a few suggestions that may help.

First: You must ask yourself the question: *Is my demand realistic? And more importantly, can they give me what I want?*

Second: *In what form am I willing to receive what I want?* In other words, am I prepared to offer terms if I get what I want?

Third: *When do I get it?*

THE THIRD SECRET PRINCIPLE:

Seek Fervently To Understand What Your Opponent Hopes To Gain From The Negotiation.

Know this first: *problems seldom exist on the level at which they are expressed.* Things are seldom what they seem. You will be far ahead if you can discover with certainty what your opponent wants. The very best way to find out is to ask. Then hear them out. When they have finished expressing themselves, repeat back to them what they said. This shows them you understand and have been listening. It also puts you in control of the conversation.

The big mistake many people make is they assume they know what the other side wants. Remember, things are seldom what they seem. *So ask.* It is one of the best ways to start the negotiating process. By asking them what they want you often create a positive atmosphere. One thing is for sure: *you certainly get their attention.*

By asking, you are, in effect, taking charge. You are in control even though they are doing most of the talking. You will get the information you need and want but, as of yet you have not revealed any of your negotiating strategies to them.

You have just stayed calm, smiled and listened. Because you have patiently and earnestly listened to their grievance and their wishes, when it comes time for you to speak they will be more apt to listen carefully to you. You now know what they want and what you want.

If you are not sure of your next response, you can simply take a break and give yourself time to digest the information you obtained while considering what to do next. This brings me to the next secret negotiating principle.

THE FOURTH SECRET PRINCIPLE:

Ask Yourself This Question,
"Is This Adversarial Situation
Really Worth The Trouble?"

Sometimes you win by simply refusing to be drawn into the fray.
Life is not about demanding to have your own way.

Life is about peace of mind
noble purpose
and striving for excellence.

Sometimes the struggle through the muck and mire of the negotiation process is not really worth pursuing. So ask yourself the question: *is this really worth the trouble?* If it is not, satisfy your opponent if you can and move on to the more important aspects of your life.

THE FIFTH SECRET PRINCIPLE:

Ask Yourself This Question
"Is This Negotiation Worth My Time?"

Many things may be worth the trouble and you may feel a great need to have a negotiated settlement but is it worth your time?

If the struggle is going to be a long one, not only taking up your time but also your energy, keeping you preoccupied when you could be working on more pleasant projects, is it worth your time? That really is a serious consideration.

Remember:

Time is what we have,
and wisdom is how we use it.

THE SIXTH SECRET PRINCIPLE:

Make Sure Your Body Language Is Working For You, Not Against You.

If you have decided the situation is worth the trouble and the time and you have pulled together your plan of action, you know what you want and what they want, and then it is on with the negotiating. A grave mistake made by many people and one to avoid at all costs is the subject of body language.

Without a doubt, if you are not aware of the signals your body sends, you can definitely hinder and even hurt your position in the negotiation process. If you are nervous, it may show and be considered a sign of weakness. You must consciously control these nervous mannerisms: shuffling your feet, tapping your fingers on a table, lowering your eyes to avoid eye contact. The list is endless.

The key is simplicity of movement. When the meeting begins, simply take your seat in a well-postured manner; be careful not to cross your arms or legs. Simply lay one hand on top of the other, either in your lap or on the table if there is one.

You may want to use your arms and hands as your speak. Otherwise, the concept *less is more* works fine. When the other side is speaking, take deep breaths. This has a calming effect. But be careful you are not noticed. Do not give yourself away.

In negotiating, nodding your head in an affirmative manner and taking notes tells your opponent you are listening and that is good. Occasionally, contact your opponent's eyes with your own and hold that contact longer than normal. In this way you are letting your body work for you not against you. At the cost of repetition it is important to remember to smile and then smile even more.

THE SEVENTH SECRET PRINCIPLE:

Be Consistently Aware Of Your Tone Of Voice. Keep It Soft, Calm but Confident.

In negotiating the voice, as much as anything, is often a very big giveaway to how you feel about the process. If you get angry, if you are not careful, your voice will reveal your anger.

If you get too worked up emotionally your voice will reveal that you are heating up. If your attitude is negative, your voice will reflect it.

Therefore, the object is to keep your emotions in check and speak softly, calmly but confidently.

Let us summarize this formula for successful negotiating so that you can see these seven secret principles in order. You will discover that you have a great plan for any situation where you have to negotiate.

Again, there are three main steps to assuring success. First, you must know yourself; you must know your opponent; you must know the differences between you.

Two: Decide exactly what you want from the negotiation.

Three: Seek fervently to understand what your opponent hopes to gain from the negotiations.

Four: Ask yourself is this situation is really worth the trouble.

Five: Ask yourself if the negotiation is truly worth your time.

Six: Make sure your body language is working for you.

Seven: Be consistently aware of your tone of voice. Keep it soft, calm and confident.

These seven negotiating secrets together with the nine basic concepts of successful negotiations will assure that you are now prepared for a future moment when you have to negotiate.

It is wonderful to be a great negotiator but it is far better to be watchful for things that may become trouble spots and solve them before they deteriorate.

The ancient proverb *an ounce of prevention is worth a pound of cure* is still wise advice for modern man.

I am happy to report that striving for success does not mean you will be constantly involved in heavy negotiations and problems, not at all. Most of your time will be spent with pleasant challenges, positive people and wonderful moments of personal growth.

However, the truly successful person knows that occasionally there comes a time when you have to take your stand, to be willing to fight for what is right.

You stand alone if need be but you stand. When that moment comes, you now have these sixteen proven secret negotiating concepts to support you. Use them along with your personal faith, with right on your side. You will overcome, success will be yours and you will enjoy the thrill of living the *Richer Life*.

*You Are Building Your Future
By The Quality Of Thinking
You're Doing Today.*

Rick C. Ernst

CHAPTER FIFTEEN

SELF-DISCIPLINE: THE ART OF PERSONAL VIRTUE

Without question, we live in an age where sociologists and psychologists vainly try to explain every possible failure. In fact, failures today are not called failures. People who fail are considered socially challenged, morally challenged, financially challenged, community challenged. The list goes on. The bottom line is that people do fail. You can call it what you will.

You can offer highly intellectual arguments for why we should not call people failures. Yet the truth is plain and simple: people do fail. There are failures in every generation.

However, in this chapter my goal is not to concentrate on failure. My goal is to provide you with insightful, key information about both failure and success so that you can make the right decisions leading to success and prosperity for you and your loved ones.

Here you will discover why so few people really succeed, why so many fail and most importantly how you can know for certain you will be counted among the successful of this generation.

Let us start with an understanding of one of the biggest success ingredients, that of self-discipline, which is actually the art of self-control. It is one of those key insights to how success occurs.

I am excited to be able to share with you three dynamic ideas that will lead you to your own personal road to success. You need to understand at the very outset that failure is self-inflicted. I want you to read that again, *failure is self-inflicted.* You are only a failure when you admit you are. As long as you are willing to pursue success, to personally discipline yourself, to master the art of self-control, in no way can your life be considered a failure.

It may take you longer than others to reach your goals, However, if you are willing to persevere, to dedicate yourself to the art of self-control through discipline, your moment will come. You will climb the mountain and stand at the peak with success and prosperity as your certificates of achievement.

I have divided this chapter into three major divisions:

One: Defining self-discipline.
Two: Understanding the value of the self-disciplined life.
Three: Acquiring the art of self-control through self-discipline.

The first thing I always notice about self-disciplined people is that they stand apart. Yes, they stand apart. I am not saying they are weird or somehow untouchable but they are definitely different. You have heard this expression: you have to learn to go with the flow.

Life does have a flow to it. But not everything in the flow of life is good for you; not everything builds you up; not everything is useful. In fact, much of the flow of life is simply transporting people to various levels of mediocrity and failure.

The self-disciplined person does not jump in; he does not participate; he knows what is good for him. If the moment does come and he is fooled and jumps in, he will soon step out again.

The self-disciplined person is not huddled with the masses at the bottom rung on the ladder of success. He finds a way up, over or around this crowd. He seeks success by following his own chosen path. Yes, he stands apart.

Another way to express what I am saying is that those who are self-disciplined, those who are acquiring the art of self-control, are rare, for instance like the American bald eagle. The eagle does not flock. Did you know that? Eagles do not flock. If you are going to go out to view eagles, you do that activity one bird at a time. In addition, eagles mate for life, unlike other feathered species. The male cares for the feeding and raising of the young eaglets, even to the point of teaching the little ones to fly. This is a rare winged creature. Because of their rare traits, they stand high above others in the wild, truly birds of beauty and destiny.

This magnificent bird seems somehow to sense his uniqueness. You will do well to follow the example of these rare birds. Stand apart. Be yourself. Stay away from the masses. Before you make a decision to jump in, check the flow. Know exactly where it is headed.

Self-discipline begins in the mind with the will. Not willpower but will. Willpower and self-control come later. You begin first of all with the ascent of the will. You demonstrate your willingness to become a self-disciplined person.

A man with a message for all who would be self-disciplined was the commander-in-chief of the Confederate troops during the Civil War. On one occasion a young mother brought her baby to General Lee to be blessed. General Lee took the infant in his arms, looked at him and then the mother and slowly said, "Teach him he must deny himself." Wow! What great advice!

Remember this point; learn to *deny yourself*, except for all things that are good for you, all things that are excellent and all things that will advance you towards the *Richer Life*.

In Charles Swindoll's book *Living Above The Level of Mediocrity*, he defines the type of self-denial that will bring success:

> "*The world needs men and I might add women who cannot be bought; Whose word is their bond; Who put*

character above wealth; Who possess opinions and a will; Who are larger than their vocations; Who do not hesitate to take chances; Who will not lose their individuality in a crowd; Who will be as honest in small things as in great things; Who will make no compromise with wrong;

Whose ambitions are not confined to their own selfish desires; Who will not say they do it 'because everybody else does it'; Who are true to their friends through good and evil report, in adversity as well as in prosperity;

Who do not believe that shrewdness, cunning and hardheadedness are the best qualities for winning success; Who are not ashamed or afraid to stand for the truth when it is unpopular; Who can say no with emphasis, although all the rest of the world says yes."

Now that is a great list of positive self-disciplining ideas! However, for me, laying aside all of the definitions I have spoken of thus far, I would say to you that people who are self-disciplined are committed to directing all of their daily energies to acquiring those talents and skills that result in total integrity and excellence of spirit.

Let us now move on to the second point:

The value of discipline.

I have seven valuable concepts to share with you and I encourage you to study and meditate upon each of them.

The first of the seven values of discipline is:

The beginning of excellence is the desire for discipline.

Down through the ages the wisdom of this proverb has been restated repeatedly. If you truly desire to be a disciplined, virtuous person, you are also on your way to being considered a wise person. These two attributes of success, discipline and wisdom, go together.

The second of the seven values of discipline is a wonderful proverb from the mind and wisdom of General George Washington, the father of our country:

> *"Discipline is the soul of an army:*
> *it makes small numbers formidable;*
> *procures success to the weak and esteem to all."*

I love the simplicity of this concept. Washington says discipline is at the very soul of the matter and he is right. Discipline is what separates victory from defeat. Discipline is like the cold steel in a mighty warrior's sword. Washington goes on to say that, small numbers of disciplined men are as a fortress. In fact, one disciplined man is worth a thousand who are not. Finally, Washington says even the weak can be shaped by discipline. Esteem and honor will eventually be theirs. If you know your American history, you know that Washington took a small number of disciplined, dedicated men and put to flight the most powerful army in the world.

The third of the seven values of discipline:

> *Discipline is the inner strength*
> *that generates self-control.*

Discipline of self puts you in control of your life. You become harnessed focused and in harmony with the laws of excellence. Above all, you are honest with yourself.

There is a great line in Shakespeare's *Hamlet* that has tremendous value if you are serious about self-control, the disciplined life. Carefully consider these next few words.

> *"This above all, to thine own self be true,*
> *and it must follow, as the night the day,*
> *thou canst not then be false to any man."*

Do you see the connection? If you are disciplined in your inner life, in your soul, if you are truthful to yourself, if you are controlled by the noble qualities of excellence, then in all that you do in life you will not only appear to be one of a few good men, you will be one.

The fourth of the seven values of discipline is:

Disciplined people direct their own energies and talents toward success and they do not rely on others to carry them along.

As I said before, disciplined people stand apart. They go where others are unwilling to go. They do what others will not do. They understand this axiom of the disciplined mind:

If you are willing to do what others will not do, you will eventually have what others will never have.

That is the secret of why disciplined people are able to enjoy much of the *Richer Life*. They do what is required. They never grumble or complain. They steel themselves against negativity and move forward at any cost. And success yields its very best to them.

The fifth of the seven values of discipline is the understanding of one of the basic laws of success motion:

A person cannot travel within and stand still without.

This is such a marvelous law of success. Often I see in my live events so many people who think that success comes from strength, from being highly educated and from skills. While strength, education and skills are great assets, many times they are not the major assets that lead to success.

Here is the secret key. A person, who travels within, is a person who knows that the greatest energy on earth is the energy released from a *disciplined mind*.

Great successful men have great minds, minds in which they travel. By that I mean they constantly search their mind, accenting the positive and eliminating the negative. They do not accept within their mind the possibility of defeat. As a result their outer life is affected dramatically. They are on the move toward success and prosperity and they soon arrive at the destination of their dreams.

The sixth of the seven values of discipline is seen in the profile of a self-disciplined person:

Disciplined people work hard
not only to acquire certain knowledge,
but they also have developed the know-how
to harness and process that knowledge into success.

I have discovered that successful people often do not have a broad-based field of knowledge. In fact many successful people I have met seemed to be very inept regarding knowledge about things in general. However, a closer look showed that when it came to their business, to their vision of success, it was obvious they worked very hard to acquire a certain great knowledge. They also had the ability to process knowledge in such a way that their life was energized and disciplined for success. In addition, I have found that disciplined people throw out the peripheral. They think and act in specifics. They control their thinking and as a result, their knowledge. Even though it may be limited or specifically focused in a given area, it keeps them moving toward full and lasting success.

Earlier in this chapter I shared with you that the desire to be disciplined or to exercise self-control in your life begins first in your mind. In other words, you *will* it to be so. Now, this will that exists in your mind, causing you to want to be disciplined, is not yet at this moment what we call *willpower*. No, at this moment, it is just the early stirring of positive thinking or we could say your *positive will*. Willpower, on the other hand, is a powerful life force for success.

It springs forth from your positive will only and I repeat, *only* when it has an *object to focus on*—in your case the desire to live a disciplined life.

As you focus on the goal to live a disciplined life, the power of your positive will or, as we can now say, your *willpower*, begins to produce the discipline and self-control you desire. This in turn will lead you to strive to excel in everything you do in your life, reaching for higher and nobler levels of success. The seventh value of discipline is:

Discipline produces the willpower to excel.

If you are one who strives to be disciplined, it is easy to understand why the ancient Greek philosophers wrote:

"Badness you can get easily, in quantity.
The road is smooth and it lies close by.

But in front of excellence the
immortal gods have put sweat,
and long and steep is the way
to it and rough at first.

When you come to the top, then
it is easy, even though it is been hard."

I can tell you with full confidence that *only the disciplined life can produce excellence.* You should also know the disciplined life is not an easy life but it is worth the effort for it leads to certain and sure accomplishment and success. Vince Lombardi said:

"Every great man loves discipline."

Before we go on, I want to recap the ground we have covered so far. Again, there are the seven great values of the self-disciplined life. How powerful and wonderful they are and before long, all of them will be part of your character and makeup.

One: The beginning of excellence is the desire for discipline.

Two: Discipline is a moral and spiritual force leading to personal strength, success and positive self-esteem.

Three: Discipline is an inner strength that promotes self-control.

Four: Disciplined people direct their own energies and talents toward success and they do not rely on others to carry them along.

Five: As you expand your mind, filling it with positive, dynamic thoughts of success, you move forward in life to success.

Six: When you live the disciplined life, you are seeking to become a person of knowledge and you know how to process this knowledge for your benefit.

Seven: Your desire to be discipline produces the willpower that leads you to a life of excellence.

Thus far, you have learned the definition of discipline and have discovered how valuable it is to you in your journey to the fulfilling world of success and prosperity. Now I want to focus on how to become a disciplined person.

There are eight secrets for acquiring and incorporating the dynamics of discipline into your life and work.

SECRET NUMBER ONE:
The Quest For The Disciplined Life Is Never Complete.

It is evident in all disciplined people that their master plan for acquiring the disciplined life allows for no vacation. They have a daily, weekly, monthly, yearly routine and they stick with it.

To develop and profit from a disciplined life is not something that you can take up and set aside whenever you wish. Once the commitment is made, the key to developing and maintaining self-discipline is the consistency of your effort.

SECRET NUMBER TWO:
All Excesses Must Be Eliminated.

This is the basic activity of all who are determined to be disciplined for success and prosperity.

Excesses exist in every aspect of life. The challenge is to be honest enough to admit them and get to work eliminating them.

The object of this exercise is to take an inventory of all things that have kept you from being totally disciplined in your life.

Once these excesses and weaknesses are identified, you begin the work of eliminating them from your life.

- *Are you a procrastinator? Change! Eliminate!*

- *Do you tend to drink too much? Change! Eliminate!*

- *Are you overweight? Change! Eliminate!*

- *Are you late for appointments? Change! Eliminate!*

- *Are you critical of others? Change! Eliminate!*

These are just a few examples of the excesses that keep a person from being a disciplined, success-oriented achiever.

Remember whatever the excess:

Change! Eliminate!

SECRET NUMBER THREE:
Discipline Requires A High Standard Of Personal Ethics.

In my lifetime I have never seen or heard a disciplined man or woman who did not also exhibit a high standard of personal ethics. Discipline and ethics go hand in hand.

When the heart is harnessed,
the work of disciplining the whole man
is not nearly as hard.

SECRET NUMBER FOUR:

Discipline Requires That
You Develop A High Energy Level.

As you become more disciplined, your energy level will increase automatically. Why? Simple: disciplined people root out the unimportant and operate instead on a well-thought-out plan of action. They do not expend their energy on trifles. Instead they reserve their energy for activities vital to their success. In that way their energy level is used wisely and profitably.

SECRET NUMBER FIVE:

The Disciplined Person Works Within The
Parameters Of A Daily, Weekly, Monthly
And Yearly Priority System.

Priorities are the yard markers of life. Establishing the priorities for each day, week, month and year is a prime method of taking control of both your mind as well as your body. Keeping the priorities of your life fresh in your mind will keep you on the straight and narrow pathway to building within you the disciplined life.

SECRET NUMBER SIX:

The Disciplined Person Is Not Afraid
Of The Risk Involved In Becoming Successful.

In the world, one views many different types of people, all being rewarded for their efforts in different ways. Some are rewarded with billions of dollars, some with millions, some with thousands and some with hundreds of dollars.

What creates this disparity? It is simple. There is a law at work in the universe that declares:

The greater the risk,
the greater the reward.

This law encompasses all of life, including the pay we receive for the work we do. The disciplined person knows this is true. You must understand that every step you take has some measurable risk. If your steps are the width of an infant's stride, the reward will be small. If your step is giant, the reward will be large.

The simple reason so many people are not living more successful lives is that they have not yet disciplined themselves to take larger steps in life. One thing is for certain: once they do, they will never retreat to the baby's stride. Therefore, your challenge is, to push yourself in using self-discipline.

Take a giant step; dare to risk. You will move forward toward your goal and an added benefit is that your growth in discipline and self-control will also increase.

SECRET NUMBER SEVEN:

Your Opportunity For Success
Is Not Determined By Fate Or Luck,
But Rather By Discipline.

Success is not a matter of *luck* but a matter of *law*. Inside the law of success, discipline plays a large part in acquiring even greater success and prosperity.

You must never lose sight of the fact that at the very moment you decide to be the captain of your own ship, the master of your own fate, your life opens up to be more disciplined than ever before.

SECRET NUMBER EIGHT:
Say No To Projects And Organizations You Are Not Interested In.

Before I delve into the value of this eighth secret concept, I want to clear up any misunderstanding that could occur over this point. I am a believer that if you are to be successful you must pay something back to the community at large that helped you succeed.

This may be your church. Social and business organizations, friends, co-workers, anyone and everyone you feel may be important to your success.

When you volunteer to serve it is like planting a seed. What you are doing will pay dividends later. The point I make here in this eighth secret concept is, carefully select the volunteer work you are going to do. Do not be afraid to say *no* to projects and organizations in which you have no interest. If you feel you cannot say *no* to certain projects, you will soon become negative about the service you are rendering and that negates the whole reason for being involved in the first place. Choose a project that fulfills you, a project that makes you feel good while you are doing it.

There are, of course, in any project a few things that may not be pleasant but whatever you do, do *not* start a project you know you dislike or have no interest. Remember:

Time is what we have, and wisdom is how we use it.

Let us review these eight secret concepts. As we do, you will begin to get an idea of how to incorporate these concepts into your life, ensuring that you will become more disciplined and as a result, a success-minded achiever.

Again, secret concept number one: *The quest for the disciplined life is never complete. There is always room to become a more disciplined person.*

Secret concept number two: *All of the negative excesses of your life must be eliminated. It will not happen overnight but with continued effort, it will happen.*

Secret concept number three: *To be disciplined is to be ruled by a high standard of ethics.*

Secret concept number four: *To live a disciplined life requires that you develop a high energy level.*

Secret concept number five: *To be disciplined you must work with a daily, weekly, monthly and yearly priority system.*

Secret concept number six: *The disciplined person is aware of and willing to take the risk involved in becoming successful.*

Secret concept number seven: *A disciplined person knows that his success is not determined by fate or luck but by the eternal laws of success.*

Secret concept number eight: *To be disciplined is to always have the courage to say no to projects and organizations in which you have no interest.*

There you have them: fifteen dynamic success concepts on how to become a more disciplined person. As you become that person, your life takes on a new dimension and you will find yourself with more confidence, more self-discipline than you ever dreamed possible.

I urge you to get started now, today. If you will, you are on your way to fulfilling all your dreams and receiving the very best life has to offer, a life called the *Richer Life.*

Chapter Sixteen

PERSISTENCE: YOUR APPRENTICESHIP TO SUCCESS

When the subject of success arises, everyone seems to have an opinion as to why certain people succeed and others do not. The list of reasons seems endless. People succeed in their endeavors for some obvious reasons.

The product or service fills a need or their endeavor was brought into being at just the right time; sometimes a product or service becomes in demand through legislation and so on.

However, when you look at the other side, that is, why people fail, in my opinion the debate never gets off the ground, because the one thing that keeps people from becoming successful has nothing to do with their lack of education, money, tools, equipment or even difficult economic times.

The number one reason why people fail to become successful is *a lack of persistence*: a failure of persistently pursuing their goals, dreams and ambitions. This is the number one reason. Here is what Webster's dictionary says about persistence:

Persistence is to continue
in a course of action without regard to
discouragement, opposition or previous failure.

It is important to recognize that persistence is first, a planned activity, a course of action. Persistence has no regard for moments of discouragement, from either within or without. Persistence does not recognize opposition. So no matter how many failures you may have had in your life, disregard the past and persist until success comes.

Whenever we see persistence in the lives of others, we admire those persons and rightfully so. Persistence is to be honored. What I am going to say next however, may surprise you, yet it is true.

Persistence, while it is an admirable trait, it is *not* a rare virtue of life. Persistence is not rare. In fact everyone, all human beings, are born with persistence, enough of it so that if they were giving out trophies, everyone would be tied for first place.

The question that needs to be answered is, if persistence is not an exceptionally rare attribute, why do only a few people in each generation demonstrate they have it? Why do so few use it to reach their goals? As I begin to answer those questions, I want to again make the point that persistence is *not* a rare quality.

At first blush, it may appear that I am mistaken, because so few people are ever persistent in any endeavor. In that context, persistence does seem as if it is a rare virtue. However, here is why I am certain I am right in declaring to you that persistence is not rare. In fact, *everyone has a large reservoir of persistence just waiting to be released.*

Just watch children and you will see the evidence of the vast amount of persistence available to human beings. We have all heard mothers and fathers say something like this to their children: "Do not ask me again. Quit pestering me."

What these mothers and fathers are saying is, "Turn your persistence-release mechanism down. You're coming on too strong." There is no doubt about it, children are persistent and they know they are. It is one of the ways they learn to get what they want. If every child has an enormous amount of persistence, enough to last a lifetime, why do most adults not exhibit this valuable trait? This is the key question.

The facts are that most children as they grow up get so many negative signals that eventually lead them to be underachievers. They are told so many times to "quit persisting; be reasonable; do not expect too much; plug into a good secure job."

Finally, little by little, the *natural* flow of persistence is blocked off by negativity and most people then go through their adult life never really understanding the significant value of the amazing, powerful attribute of persistence. It is repressed and it remains so until they catch a new vision for life, a vision that is so positive, so strong in their mind that the negative dam holding back a flood of persistence is broken and persistence, once again, flows naturally in, around and through their life.

In this chapter, I will lead you through ten exciting secret concepts, ways and means to unlock deeper levels of persistence for your life and for your success, now and in the future. I challenge you to take each of these ten concepts seriously and incorporate their value into your life. If you do, persistence will soon be one of your most dynamic strengths.

THE FIRST SECRET CONCEPT:
Find A Positive Mission For Your Life.

The reason most people have limited amounts of persistence in their lives is very simple. *They have nothing in their lives that requires them to be persistent.* Therefore, the first and truly the most important step is to find a mission for your life.

All great thinkers have understood that life will remain shallow, unchallenged and remote, until you dream a lofty dream, the so-called impossible dream. To have a dream, a vision—that is what a mission for life is all about. If you have never allowed yourself to be challenged by the thrill of an exciting big dream, today is the day to begin and today is the day persistence will become your ally.

THE SECOND SECRET CONCEPT:
Crystallize Your Mission, Your Vision Into Specific Goals.

If you take the time to really think about it, a vision for life is at first a want, a wish. Here are a few examples. *I want to be happy.* That is a wish. However, when you answer the question *what will make me happy?* Now you have a goal. See how that works? Here is another one: *I want to make a lot of money.* That is a vision you may have for your life. You crystallize the vision into a goal by answering the question, *what service will I offer that will make me a lot of money?*

Now you have a mission for life. Let me give you one more. *I want to travel.* That is a vision. You will crystallize that want into a goal by asking the questions, *where do I want to travel? When will I go? How much money is required?* And so on.

Your vision, your dream, your mission, must be crystallized into a specific goal. The good news is:

Knowing your destination is half the journey.

Once you know what you want to do, have and become, your storehouse of persistence will open. The power to persist until you reach your goal will be given.

THE THIRD SECRET CONCEPT:
Develop A Master Plan Of Action That Allows You To Complete Your Goals.

Now that your goals are clearly defined, the next step is to get some wheels under your goals so that you can move forward. That is what a plan of action does for you.

No football coach would ever send his team onto the field without a plan of action or to put it in football jargon, a game plan. The game plan may be modified as the game goes on but it is extremely important that there be a game plan or in your case, a master plan of action set forth at the very beginning.

A plan of action will assist you in allocating your time and energy in the correct manner. You will be moving forward on purpose and with persistence. You will find that other people's actions will not determine your priorities. You are now organized for action. You will also be more effective in the use of your time because your work activity is laid out in advance. It has been proven repeatedly. The more advance planning you have done, the less total time is required to complete the project. That is just part of the value of a well-thought-out master plan of action.

Yes, it takes courage to push yourself to places that you have never been before, to test your limits, to break through barriers. Yet all that and more you will do on the road to success. And a master plan of action is a great tool to see you through.

THE FOURTH SECRET CONCEPT:
Practice Being Persistent.

As a rule, most of your daily activities will not call for great sacrifice, extreme determination or all-out persistence. Most of your daily work will be steady, calm, sometimes even boring.

Yet when all is said and done, most of the time the *small daily triumphs* ultimately result in achieving exceptional success in life. Along the way, you will find greater and greater opportunities for you to practice being persistent. I have found in my career that being persistent in the *small* moments of life does help in being persistent when the *major* moments occur.

Here is a way you can start to practice being persistent. Each day, arise and say aloud, *"I am persistent. It is impossible for me to fail."* At first, this may seem strange.

Nevertheless, remember:

The mind completes
the picture you put into it.

The successful people I know have learned the eight *Ps* of success. How about you? Do you know and practice the eight *Ps*? You should. Here they are:

- ### *Prepare - Prayerfully*

- ### *Plan - Purposefully*

- ### *Proceed - Positively*

- ### *Pursue - Persistently*

All eight of these *Ps* are extremely important but those I want to single out are the seventh and eighth *Ps*, *pursue persistently.*

From the moment you awaken, whatever activities are itemized on your daily priority list, pursue the completion of these activities persistently. Do not allow yourself to be sidetracked. Stay at it; practice being the most persistent person who ever lived. Preparing prayerfully, planning purposefully and proceeding positively.

All of these concepts are important; however, they need the clincher to make them complete. The clincher is to *pursue persistently.*

Prayerfully preparing to be successful, planning to be successful and proceeding down a predetermined pathway to success. These are important activities, to be sure but without persistence a moment will come when your path may be filled with all sorts of difficulty. You will need an extra boost of energy. This is when persistence saves the day. When nothing else will, persistence keeps you moving toward the completion of your goals. As outdated as many think Aesop's fables are, history proves the turtle can beat the rabbit. As Aesop says, *slow and steady wins the race*. This is the value of persistence. It keeps on going and going and going!

Another example of the value of persistence can be seen in a survey taken by the Retail Dry Goods Association of America. The association discovered that 48 percent of the sales representatives made a single sales call on a prospect and never tried again for a sale.

Twenty-five percent made two sales calls, 15 percent made three sales calls and 12 percent made four or more sales calls. The sales representatives who made four or more calls, those persistent few, sold 80 percent of all the dry goods sold. Need I say more?

You must be persistent;
It is simply a winner's way of life.

Some people read a book like this and wrongfully assume the author has always been a tremendous success. Well, a personal note here will shed some light on this error. Early in my career I was called on to demonstrate my own personal persistence. My goal was to enter the real estate profession. One of the prerequisites was to obtain a real estate license, normally not easy to do but certainly attainable with some effort.

For me, however, it was a different story. The Real Estate Commission administered the real estate exam only once a month, which meant that if I failed, I would have to wait an entire month before trying again.

It is not uncommon for a large percentage of the applicants to fail at their first attempt but most pass on their second try. However, this was not the situation in my case. A passing grade did not come my way until I had taken the exam *six* times. You may ask, "Well, did you not study?" Oh yes, I studied, very hard. In fact, you could ask me just about any question on the entire exam and I could give you the right answer. However, when I read the questions to myself, I could not come up with the right answers.

When I was in the second grade, I was diagnosed with dyslexia, a learning and reading disability. In those days reading was very difficult for me. Since that time, I have studied hard and with the help of specially trained reading teachers have overcome my reading problem for the most part. However, to this day I still have difficulty with some things. But I make it a priority to never look at what I *do not have*; only what I *do have*. Again, I say:

It is not the ability you have that makes you successful;

It is how you see and use your ability that determines your success.

The point I want to make about the real estate examination is that it took me six months to get my real estate license when most people do it in six weeks. However, my goal was to get my real estate license and I did. I then went on to become very successful in not only residential sales but also in selling multi-million-dollar international resort properties.

Yes, I can tell you from my own experience, persistence is the apprenticeship to success. Whatever is in your life today that is hard, difficult or not going your way, my challenge to you is, see it as an opportunity to demonstrate your persistence.

Remember this little five-word success axiom:

Get started; do not quit.

Do not miss the opportunity before you today. Apply yourself. Hang in there. Stay tough! If your resolve is firm, your desire intent, your goals crystal-clear, success will soon be your companion.

THE FIFTH SECRET CONCEPT:
Be Adaptable.

We live in a world where situations change so rapidly that while we may be unaffected one day, the next day we may be swamped with the turn of events. That is when you need what I have chosen to call *persistent adaptability*. This age we live in calls for people to be firm in their conviction, persistent in their drive for success but adaptable to new possibilities that present themselves at a moment's notice.

Here are eight ideas that I use not only in my personal life but also in leading and managing my companies. If you incorporate them into your life, they will assist you in acquiring the great virtue of persistent adaptability.

One: *View change as normal.*

One thing is for certain: things change, sometimes for the better, sometimes for the worse. Even the most solid of relationships, financial conditions and corporate stability undergo change that can shock everyone involved.

I have the privilege to work with a good many top executives in my success coaching practice and one sentiment I hear more and more is "I can't believe it; I never expected this to happen to me; I wasn't prepared for it." What I am suggesting to you is, expect the unexpected. Be ready for change in all the ways you can. That is the cornerstone of persistent adaptability.

Two: *Do not lock yourself in; be ready for change.*

Years ago the following advice was given to young men and women seeking to become successful. The wisdom of that age said, "Put all your eggs in one basket and watch that basket."

The idea was to lock yourself in, find a secure niche and stay there. They were told, "Whatever you do, stay with the job." In the early 1900s through the 1970s, it was common to spend a whole career with one corporation. To stay with one corporation was to be responsible, to be a solid citizen of the community. However, beginning in the late 1970s the eggs-in-the-basket philosophy shifted 180 degrees.

The advice then turned to; do not put all your eggs in one basket. Be flexible. Watch for opportunities to move up the ladder of success, even if it means switching from one corporation to another. Still, no matter the route you choose, persistence will be required.

Three: *Stay on the straight and narrow road to success.*

By watching and coaching people over the years, I have come to understand why many with great talent and ability fail to succeed. They allow themselves to detour from their vision and goals. They become bogged down in trifles. As one person put it, *they major in minors.* You will discover as I have that to stop your quest for success, to change every little thing that goes awry is not worth the effort. The key is to keep your mind centered on the larger vision.

Remember, complete the number one priority of each day; then there will be time to fix the little things that irritate you. Be persistent in the big picture and often the little things take care of themselves.

Four: *Be creative; find ways to be more efficient.*

Most of the time, no matter what goal we choose, we run on a success track staked out by those who have gone before us. And it is right that we do. But not everything others have done will work for you. You may have to blaze a new trail, invent new ways on your own. Persistent people innovate. They investigate. They find a way.

On those rare occasions they cannot change something, they adapt. Therefore, persistent adaptability is the key to your success, now and in the future.

Five: ***Do not become disheartened or discouraged by the lack of immediate results.***

I have spoken of Dr. William James in other chapters and here I have taken a sentence from his essay *The Will to Believe*.

> ***"Often our faith in an uncertified result is the only thing that makes the results come true."***

In this sentence, Dr. James reveals to us why, in great endeavors, we never allow ourselves to become discouraged. Instead we persist, no matter how dark the storm clouds in our life appear. There is a great secret locked up in this small sentence.

Your faith, aided by a persistent effort to achieve success, may be all you have going for you but as Dr. James says, that is enough. *Faith plus persistence creates positive results.*

You may be saying, "You're asking me to take a great risk if you are asking me to step out on faith alone." That is true. There is a risk involved. However, I can promise you this: when you act upon your faith, it will always release persistence and persistence will lead you to the moment when positive results begin to appear.

Faith and persistence fight discouragement. Faith and persistence protect you from the negativity that would like to steal your progress. In the beginning, remember, faith and persistence may indeed be all you have going for you but empires have been built on these two words. You can trust these two virtues.

Faith and persistence will keep you going and eventually the success you desire will flow forth into your life.

Six: ***Do not be discouraged by major setbacks.***

I have yet to meet a person who has achieved success in life easily without risk and setback and, above all, doggedly persisting to complete the goals of their life. Wise men and women expect setbacks. They come with the territory.

One of the basic reasons you will encounter one or more major setbacks is, in the beginning, you lack experience. In the beginning, it is all new. You are not always sure which way to proceed. For things to go wrong is normal. Our modern society has even coined a name for it: Murphy's Law, which states: *"whatever can go wrong will go wrong."*

In the beginning of your success adventure, all kinds of things will go wrong because of your inexperience but you persist, you keep on keeping on. Little by little, you will become more and more experienced and those things that happened to you in the past will not happen anymore. You persisted, you gained experience and now persistent effort has made you wiser. You now have the upper hand. Yes, persistence will play a great role not only in the beginning but also throughout your entire success journey.

The commitment to be persistent will lead you on to greater and greater steps to personal success. In time your persistence will give you an even greater boldness for life. You will be more confident of yourself. Things that would have been major setbacks in the past are now handled with wisdom and persistence.

Seven: *Do not be discouraged by the negativity of others.*

My experience has shown that if you strive to get ahead, if you really attempt to make something out of your life, the voices of negativity will echo about you. Often, strange as it is, these negative voices will be those people closest to you: loved ones, relatives, best friends. Somehow these people always think they are doing you a favor by pointing out all the things that can go wrong.

For sure, they have a genuine desire to keep you from making a mistake. However, if you are not careful, they will be convincing and you will be turned away from a great adventure, the adventure of following your own personal dream or vision of success.

Eight: *Develop an inner circle.*

By an inner circle I mean a few steadfast, positive friends. We all need positive people in our lives. You need people to emulate, people to admire for their persistent efforts, people who can give you wise counsel. In short, you need positive people in your life who believe in you and can encourage you when times get tough. It goes without saying that these people should be available whenever the need arises. In his book *The Winning Attitude*, John Maxwell describes four virtues to look for in the people that you allow in your inner circle.

First, this must be someone who loves you and who is a positive encourager. When a person demonstrates their love for you and constantly seeks to encourage you, this will flood into your life in a wonderful way and it will help you grow more and more persistent in your efforts to be successful. Your confidence will grow; your faith will expand. You will work harder not only because you do not want to fail yourself but you want to live up to the vision your friend has of you.

Second, an inner circle person must be someone with whom you have mutual honesty and transparency. This is a rare bond between two people. However, when it happens and when it is real, there is a synergistic contact of the spirit and both lives are blessed.

Third, an inner circle person must be someone who is already successful in overcoming challenges and opportunities. You do not need a cheerleader; you need a leader, period. You need someone who can provide the right example or share their experience with you, someone who can say with confidence, "Here's what you should do."

Fourth, an inner circle person must have a strong faith in God and be someone who believes in miracles.

People who have *no* faith in the immediacy of God can help you when times are good but they will have nothing to offer when your life is dry, when in your spirit, you are on the backside of the desert, unable to right yourself. Only then, can the spiritual man counsel.

Frankly, the unbeliever just waits for circumstances to change. The man of faith can, by prayer and faith in God, rule circumstances.

Throughout my career I have been able to make sales, get contracts signed and do other things at times and places that no one else could. On many occasions I have out-negotiated big-name negotiators; I have won in situations where the odds were dead set against me.

You may ask how I have done all this. What is my big secret? Well, my secret is one, wise counsel from my inner circle and two, which is even more important, is what I call *KP*. Yes *KP*. What is *KP*? *Knee Power*. That is right, I have prayed in these situations. One of the Bible verses I rest on when change is required in any situation is Proverbs 21:1.

> ***The king's heart is in the hand of the Lord.***
> ***He directs it like a water course***
> ***wherever he pleases.***

The Bible says God hears the prayers of a righteous man. So once again, when selecting your inner circle, make certain they are people of strong faith. The question is often asked: "where do you find such people?" The answer will be different for each person. These people may already be in your life and you just have not yet asked them to help. You may find them in your church, at work, among your membership associations or even relatives.

If you cannot find them, begin at once to pray that God will provide you a few success warriors. In time, the ones you need will surface. In addition, I suggest you make a commitment to always follow the free enterprise code of persistence.

The eight principles of the free enterprise code of persistence were first printed in a slightly different form in Harold Sherman's book *How to Turn Failure into Success*. I have made them fit a free enterprise model for success, the same free enterprise system that has given rise to the publication of this book.

The first principle: *I will never quit persisting when I know that what I am doing is right.*

The second principle: *I will persist daily, praying and believing that all things will work out for me.*

The third principle: *I will be courageous, undismayed and persistent in the face of all odds.*

The fourth principle: *I will not permit anyone or anything to intimidate me or deter me from persistently working to complete my goals.*

The fifth principle: *I will not be discouraged I will persist again and again until I accomplish my goals.*

The sixth principle: *With my persistence, I will see a setback as a setup to succeed.*

The seventh principle: *I will persistently persist. I know that all successful people have had to fight adversity and failure. I will follow the pathway they have unselfishly blazed for me.*

The eighth principle: *I will never surrender to discouragement or despair. I will persist until all obstacles are completely conquered.*

Now you possess these specific ideas on how persistence works to help you to achieve all the success you desire. It has been proven that each of these concepts will help to release tremendous amounts of persistence in your life and work.

I leave you with a small credo that thousands upon thousands of success-achieving people have based their efforts and their lives on. Consider carefully the message of Calvin Coolidge, the thirtieth president of the United States. In studying the subject of persistence, he wrote this message just for you. Here it is:

Press on. Nothing in the world can take the place of persistence. Talent will not. Nothing is more common than unsuccessful men with talent.

Genius will not. Unrewarded genius is almost a proverb.

Education will not. The world is full of educated derelicts.

Persistence and determination alone are omnipotent.

It simply cannot be said any better. You can count on it; *persistence is the apprenticeship to success.*

As I have said before:

Success is your birthright, failure is your option.

It is true, success and prosperity is your infinite right. Remember, *do not* live your life based on how you *feel*; live your life based on what you *know*.

Now that you *know* these proven success principles, make them your own by putting them to work in your life. When you do, success is in your future. Yes, success is your destiny. So start today, right now!

Reach out and take the life you want; I have done it, others have done it and now it is your turn to make your mark. You are now prepared. You *know* the dynamic success ingredients. You *know* the *Richer Life Secrets.*

To Think Is To Create:

Therefore,
Create . . .
The Life You Want.

Rick C. Ernst

An Interview With
Rick C. Ernst

The below questions and answers have been assembled from various sources such as Rick C. Ernst's TV and talk radio appearances, speaking engagements and nationwide telephone conference calls.

~

Q: I have heard testimonies about the remarkable results participants experience at the Richer Life Experience. I am wondering how you can help people fix their problems and multiply their incomes so fast when other experts claim these things take time?

RCE: In the Richer Life Experience, instead of spending time in trying to solve the symptoms of problems, I teach participants to discern their root problems and then I coach them to take the most appropriate cure or actions to rectify their personal and financial issues.

~

Q: I've read that your services include the coaching of celebrities, top-level corporate leaders and other successful individuals. Why would they need a success coach? Aren't they already successful?

RCE: In working with these "successful" individuals, my experience as a Life Success Coach has revealed that prominent, high-profile individuals are uniquely challenged in finding qualified professionals to coach them through their professional dilemmas and obstacles as well as their private life issues. Few people can really understand and relate to the problems and situations almost all these outstanding achievers and public figures encounter.

Q: *I am a regional director, will attending the Richer Life Experience help me to improve my corporate management teams?*

RCE: Most definitely. I recommend you bring as many of your team members as possible to the live event. The bonding and synergistic alignment will have a tremendous impact on each individual and your team as a whole.

~

Q: *I have a home based business and I'm interested in increasing my profits. What can the Richer Life Experience provide in this area?*

RCE: There are five ways to increase profit:

1.   Increase the number and quality of customers.

2.   Increase the amount of business with each individual customer.

3.   Reduce or eliminate marketing cost.

4.   Increase referral and repeat business.

5.   Do Everything Better.

I can confidently say the Richer Life Experience will be a tremendous personal growth experience for you thereby allowing you to improve and be much more effective at all of the above.

~

Q: *What moral values or religious beliefs do you encourage your participants to have or adopt?*

RCE: I do not view my position as a judge or a dictator forcing my own personal belief system on live event participants. However, as a life success coach I do feel it is my responsibility to share the truth of successful business, personal as well as spiritual principles to the best of my ability and then allow Richer Life Experience participants to make their own decisions.

Q: *I am seeking to become financially independent. The last 3 years I have enjoyed a steady increase of income but now I am ready to move up to the millionaire status level. Is your Richer Life Experience what I am looking for?*

RCE: The 3-day Richer Life Experience is attended by people from all over the world who are seeking to substantially increase their incomes. During the event, you will learn how to think like a millionaire, discover a proven formula for eliminating your debts and learn how to become financially independent.

~

Q: *Our marriage is on the rocks and we are contemplating separation. Is your live event geared towards marital counseling or is it more for those seeking general success principles?*

RCE: The Richer Life Experience is not specifically oriented towards marital issues however; the general success principles, which are taught, include building and maintaining both personal and professional relationships. Many couples have found their own marriages have been greatly enhanced by applying the relationship principles, which they received at the event.

~

Q: *I am a successful executive but feel I am losing my focus, interest, drive and desire. Maybe I am going through the so-called male mid-life crisis. I am wondering, do top-level male executives experience the so-called, "male mid-life crisis?"*

RCE: Studies indicate approximately 88 percent of male executives between 35 and 45 years of age experience a mid-life trauma of some degree. In my own coaching practice, I have found this especially true among highly motivated, very driven, successful business and professional men. I address these issues in the 3-day

Richer Life Experience, which I encourage you to attend. I am confidant you will be absolutely delighted with your experience.

~

Q: My husband is incarcerated. I am wondering if, as a success coach, do you work with prisoners in penitentiaries?

RCE: I have on several occasions, however specifically in the areas of pre-parole society adjustment.

~

Q: So many people today seem to be suffering from anxiety and depression. Do you believe in using medication for depression?

RCE: Yes I do, medication certainly has its place. However, I am of the opinion that many individuals who are on medication for depression either have been misdiagnosed or have not received adequate help or counseling.

~

Q: I'm a female executive who makes considerably more money than my husband and this has led to many problems in our marriage. Does your live event address these kinds of issues?

RCE: Yes, your situation is common among high paid female executives and must be handled in the proper way. However, it can be quickly rectified. In the Richer Life Experience, I devote a great deal of time to addressing wealth-building principles, which certainly include the proper handling of money, which would address your situation.

Let me encourage both you and your husband to attend this life-changing event; not only will your issue be cured but your entire marriage will be reinvigorated and your romance rekindled.

Q: *I was abused as a child and to this day, no one knows. Would your Richer Life Experience help me in this area?*

RCE: The Richer Life Experience is a high impact, interactive, multi-sensory, fast-paced personal growth experience. While it is impossible to address every single experience that people may encounter in life, at the live event you will discover *how to release negative issues of the past, plan for the future and live in the present.* If you are ready to take hold of your life and become the person that you are capable of being enroll now for the next live event.

~

Q: *I am in senior management. I love my work, my wife and all my children. About a week ago, my wife burst into tears and said she felt I didn't need her anymore, which is not true. How can I convince her?*

RCE: I frequently hear variations of your story, sometimes from the executive and other times from the spouse. Your situation is very common with male high achievers and there are two things you can do immediately and four things to be done long-term, which will rectify your problem. I cover this and much more, you will find very interesting and insightful in the Richer Life Experience. Your issue can be corrected however; time is not on your side. I recommend that you and your wife attend the live event as soon as possible.

~

Q: *I am 47 years old and after 22 years of employment with the same company, I was unexpectedly laid off due to cutbacks. A friend of mine recently suggested attending your event but I feel perhaps that I should try to find another job before I go to a self-improvement program. Do you think this is right?*

RCE: As a success coach I make it practice to never make decisions for people but rather to point out what options they have available and then encourage them in making a timely decision. Your options are as you say "to go and find another job or to attend the Richer Life Experience as soon as possible." When you attend the live event, your current mindset, self-confidence as well as self-esteem will be increased and your overall success consciousness will be enlarged.

In addition, the wealth building principles I will teach you during the event will open doors of opportunities that may otherwise have never presented themselves. These doors have lead many to total financial independence and my guess is these opportunities would have never been possible in your previous employment. To me the choice is obvious. Here is a hint; I look forward to meeting you at the Richer Life Experience.

~

Q: *I feel trapped, suppressed and in a rut.*

RCE: So have many other people who have attended the Richer Life Experience. Their lives are now filled with passion and purpose. At the live event, I will coach you on immediate steps, which can be taken to overcome your situation, as well as positive approaches that will influence your life and fill you with real hope for the future.

~

Q: *I'm seeking a success coach that can help me with my situation. I am in love with two different people and don't know what to do.*

RCE: This can be confusing, however, there is a way to know how to handle it and make the right decision. During the Richer Life Experience, I teach participants that our life represents an unfolding of our previous choices and decisions.

Making wise decisions is a skill that can be learned and one that you can obtain by attending the Richer Life Experience.

Q: I'm unhappy and very discontent with life but I have every material possession that anyone could ever want. Can your Richer Life Experience help me?

RCE: Yes, I have had many people in very similar circumstances attend the Richer Life Experience. They are happy and are now enjoying peace of mind.

~

Q: I feel good about my life and I am enjoying many of its rewards and pleasures but I'm always looking to grow. Would your live event help me in reaching my full potential?

RCE: Most definitely! The Richer Life Experience delivers the latest and most current life success coaching and wealth building strategies and techniques to enhance your personal and professional effectiveness allowing you to develop and maintain your winning edge for living the richer life.

~

Q: We are having severe teenage, marital and family problems in our home. We have sought much counseling but it has been of little or no help. Would attending your event be of any help or is this not appropriate for your events.

RCE: Unfortunately, I have heard many questions such as yours. Without criticizing the counselors, you have experienced or without elaborating on the Richer Life Experience, let me simply say those individuals who have attended the live event with similar circumstances are happy now.

~

Q: *Tell me more about your one-on-one life success coaching.*

RCE: It is lonely at the top - *Often high profile individuals have personal or professional issues, which they may not wish to confide to their families, co-workers or even their professional associates or counsel. My highly specialized life success coaching sessions form a behind-the-scenes alliance that assures confidentiality in an atmosphere of trust and integrity.*

This coaching is particularly suitable for those who prefer success coaching on an individual and discreet basis - such as high-profile executives, officers of public corporations politicians, professional athletes, television/motion picture personalities and other celebrities.

~

Q: *I've made my fortune and seem to have lost my drive; as a matter of fact, I'm downright bored with my business. Do you have any suggestions?*

RCE: Once financial issues have been conquered, your situation becomes a common scenario. Throughout the years, I have encountered this with other clients in my coaching practice. The great news is your situation is easily rectified.

Attending the Richer Life Experience will definitely help you overcome this and then your life, relationships and career will become exciting, challenging and rewarding once again!

~

Rick C. Ernst

Preparing You Today
For Tomorrow's Success

www.TheBestCoach.com

Live Events Conducted By Rick C. Ernst

Richer Life Experience
3 Days

As a special thank-you for purchasing *Richer Life Secrets* for a limited time, Rick C. Ernst is offering two complimentary tickets for you and a family member or friend to attend his 3-day *Richer Life Experience*. The total value of this complimentary admission for you and a companion is $3,000.

The *Richer Life Experience* delivers the latest and most current life success coaching, wealth building information and techniques. As a participant, you will discover how to achieve your ultimate personal and professional goals and experience the profound fulfillment you desire and deserve. You will learn the secrets to enhancing your overall effectiveness and satisfaction allowing you to develop and maintain an extraordinary quality of life. You will be empowered with a clear understanding of what it is you really want most in your life, relationships and career. People from all over the world who are looking to make a positive difference in their personal and professional lives attend this spectacular three-day experience.

During the *Richer Life Experience*, you will learn:

- *To think like a millionaire*

- *How to eliminate your debts and recondition your mind for wealth and financial abundance*

- *A revolutionary new process of establishing effective and compelling specific goals and how to achieve them much faster*

- *Why some people rise to the pinnacle of success in spite of tremendous obstacles while others do not*

Attending this live event will be three of the most empowering, educational and entertaining days of your life. You will identify with absolute precision what it is you really want to do, have and become. In addition, you will discover how to permanently break through any barriers that are holding you back. You will learn how to apply the specific tools and strategies for turning your dreams into reality.

As doctors operate on eyes with the precision of laser surgery, during the *Richer Life Experience* you will witness first hand your own life being changed as Rick C. Ernst operates on your thoughts and thought processes with equal precision, preparing you to achieve immediate, outstanding personal and professional results.

This event is for people who have always wanted to think, live and create like a millionaire. When you complete this exciting and insightful three-day journey, you will have transformed your thought process and have a new ability to go far beyond your current thinking. You will have a new Millionaire Consciousness and Mindset you will be free to create new and unique solutions to previously unsolvable problems from an entirely new prospective; free to create new possibilities and new opportunities.

The *Richer Life Experience* is truly a life-changing event for anyone and everyone, business people, entrepreneurs, singles, married couples, parents, teenagers and grandparents. People from all lifestyles attend this one-of-kind experience. Participants leave this event with a new clarity of mind, a new vision, purpose and tools to create the life of their dreams and enjoy living the *Richer Life*.

Transformation
3 Days

The *Transformation* event is a fast-paced, in-depth life-changing three-day event, which provides proven techniques and insights that allow you to build the kind of life, relationships and career you desire.

During the *Transformation* event, you will expand your effectiveness and deepen your satisfaction in all areas of your life.

You will learn to make thoughtful, successful and intellectual choices, relating to family, friends and business associates, as well as position your life to make a significant difference to others.

The Transformation event will teach you how to:

- *Use the proven success strategies from others and model them to replicate the same results in your own life*

- *Take control of your ultimate destiny and understand how to shape your life, relationships and career*

- *Eliminate procrastination, self-sabotage and create unstoppable self-confidence and self-esteem*

- *To improve and deepen your present relationships though effective communication*

- *Create the energy and vitality that you desire in your life*

You will return home from the *Transformation* event with a new approach and spirit towards your daily routines and commitments.

Your life will have a new sense of enthusiasm, confidence, wisdom and an overall peace, which will greatly expand your enjoyment of living the *Richer Life*.

Vertical Living
2 Days

The *Vertical Living* live event is a very popular unique, two day, spirit-filled event that crosses all denominational boundaries. You discover fresh insights uniquely presented from the word of God.

As a participant, you will be led by the Holy Spirit in discovering your calling, mission and gifts, bringing you to a deeper walk in your Christian faith.

In addition, you will learn to approach your daily challenges with a new meaning of the word commitment and the personal power that brings to your life.

During this event, you will learn how to:

- *Discover God's will for your life*

- *Live within God's plan to receive prosperity*

- *Re-building and/or strengthening relationships*

- *Close communication gaps and/or restoring marriages*

- *Overcome addictions such as smoking, drugs and over-eating, fear, rejection, anxiety, bitterness, depression*

- *Recover from a severe loss, divorce or death of a loved one*

The *Vertical Living* live event launches you on an in-depth journey of using a spiritual approach to Christian wisdom leading to God's success formulas.

If you are seeking the secrets to unlocking the power of the Holy Spirit; to experience a fuller, *Richer Life* in Jesus Christ then this two day event is a must attend.

Maximum Health
3 Days

All success coaches would certainly agree that a pure, vibrant, healthy body structure is the core foundation for achieving peak performance and fulfillment in everything you do. How can you reap the benefits of a rewarding career, financial success and loving relationships if your body is too ill, tired or weak to enjoy them?

The *Maximum Health* event delivers the learning essentials and knowledge you need for attaining and maintaining excellent health, nutrition and overall wellness. During this action-packed event, you will enjoy three interactive days of fun learning activities wherein you will acquire the wisdom and skills to completely take charge of your own health and wellness.

You will learn how to connect the science of good health with the daily activity of living in our fast-pasted society and how to totally eliminate the fear and confusion of excellent health.

You will discover exactly what to do and what not to do in order to:

- *Enjoy more energy and sleep better at night*

- *Boost your immune system*

- *Feel tremendous once again*

- *Incredibly enhance and improve your sex life at any age*

- *Eliminate the expensive pills, potions and lotions*

- *Have a slimmer, firmer body*

At the *Maximum Health* event you will learn to create the proper mind-set for lasting physical change and transform your thinking about how your physical body works and what is good for it to maintain excellent health, nutrition and overall wellness.

Passion, Purpose and Destiny
3 Days

The *Passion, Purpose and Destiny* event is an experiential three day event designed to create a safe insightful personal growth atmosphere for participants. This event uses a series of fun and insightful demonstrations, fast-paced mental drills to help you discover your personal passion, purpose and destiny.

This personal growth event is uniquely designed so that participants receive exactly what they need in their individual lives, relationships and careers. If you know in your heart that you were put on earth for more than getting up going to work, coming home and repeating the same routine day-after-day then this event is for you.

If you:

- *Are plagued by unrest and would like to feel more peaceful*

- *Feel like you can never get ahead and need direction*

- *Have the feeling that there has to be more to life than this*

- *Feel unhappy or sad about choices you have made in life and are ready to make positive changes in your life*

- *Are not doing what you would like to do to make money*

- *Have reached a junction in life and need new direction*

The Passion, Purpose and Destiny event is for you if you are ready to:

- *Reactivate the dreamer in you*

- *Rediscover the passion in you*

- *Reignite the purpose in you*

- *Reposition yourself for your success destiny*

Leadership For The 21st Century
3 Days

It is a proven fact, those individuals who possess strong leadership skills are always among the people who enjoy the highest income levels. During this insightful event, you will quickly learn the skills necessary to enhance your income and develop leadership excellence that will take you to the top personally and professionally.

Excellent leadership and communication skills go hand-in-hand with future successes. It does not matter how compelling the vision you have put forward or how brilliant your strategies have been thought through, without solid leadership there is no execution and subsequently no positive results.

This results oriented leadership event has been designed to quickly strengthen and positively reinforce your leadership communication skills. You will discover proven leadership techniques that will aid you to initiate and stimulate change, inspire, persuade and influence friends and business associates.

During the three day, Leadership For The 21st Century event you will learn how to:

- *Maximize your leadership communication skills to lead, motivate and inspire others*

- *Project a more dynamic personal/professional image*

- *Overcome communication anxiety and acquire the skills of a top effective leader to earn the respect, loyalty and trust of everyone you meet*

- *Develop a leadership style that produces amazing results in effectively dealing with problems, crises and other very difficult leadership situations*

Pillars of Personal Development
Live Event and Home Study
Coaching Series
2 Days

This popular two-day, high impact live event delivers a dynamic and effective curriculum by working in conjunction with a result driven, ongoing home study personal growth coaching series.

The live event and the home study material are independently structured to stand-alone; therefore, it is not necessary to complete one before beginning the other.

The insightful home study material of this program is delivered through interactive emails and on-demand audio recordings over the course of one full year.

In this unique personal development live event and home study success coaching series, Rick C. Ernst focuses on what he calls *Pillars of Personal Development.*

Entrepreneurship - Stress Management

Great Relationships - Motivating People

Successful Negotiations - Public Speaking

Containing the wisdom of the ages, this life success-coaching program is a one-of-a-kind program, which delivers to you a foundation of over 30-years of meticulous research and development.

It has been hailed by individuals, corporate leaders and entrepreneurs worldwide as a *must-have blueprint for success.*

The *Pillars of Personal Development* program has helped people of all ages and backgrounds absolutely leap from where they were to where they wanted to be!

Effective Communications and Public Speaking

3 Days

The three-day on your feet, *Effective Communications and Public Speaking* event will equip you with the information and skills you need to make your presentations reflect your newfound *power at the podium.*

You will learn how to organize your thoughts and develop razor sharp techniques and exciting new concepts to assist you in delivering more powerful, effective presentations, training sessions and vibrant speeches.

You will become more effective as a presenter, persuader, informer, trainer and motivator, mastering the necessary skills that are imperative to be a successful public speaker and communicator.

While attending this event, you will have the opportunity to practice and perfect insightful presentation strategies and techniques in non-threatening real life experiences by having the opportunity to speak on your feet on several occasions.

You will receive individual, personal one-on-one instruction provided by Rick C. Ernst and Richer Life Connection senior instructors and instructor staff.

Company presidents, public relations specialists, trainers, coaches, marketing VP's, salespeople, professional speakers, MLM leaders, engineers, politicians, lawyers, educators, production supervisors, bankers, human resource professionals among others benefit from this popular event.

Once you attend, we are sure you will agree this three-day training is the most comprehensive, how-to, public speaking event available anywhere. It will pay rich, positive dividends for you year after year.

Secrets To Real Estate Wealth
4 Days

At last you can learn the secrets to becoming a wealthy real estate investor even if you have *no cash* or even *bad credit*. In today's business and economic climate, people are wanting or being forced to make multiple career changes. Some due to the right sizing, down sizing or even the capsizing of their employers.

In addition, many people are seeking to leave the corporate rat race to enjoy the liberty of becoming their own boss and finally being financially rewarded for what they are worth.

At the *Secrets To Real Estate Wealth* 4-Day event you can start to make your dreams a reality by learning how to be a successful real estate investor.

Now you can learn how to buy and sell single-family homes from a proven success coach who routinely has multiple closings per month earning $25,000, $30,000, $50,000 and even over $100,000 per real estate transaction. You can even do this with *NO Cash* or even *Bad Credit*!

At the *Secrets To Real Estate Wealth* 4-Day event you are entitled to the benefit of valuable personalized coaching with Rick C. Ernst who has over 30 years of experience in investing and selling residential properties nation-wide as well as international multi-million dollar commercial real estate transactions.

During this event Rick C. Ernst will reveal to you his most coveted secrets honed over decades of testing and retesting for purchasing, with No Money Down, single family homes using the techniques of short sales, foreclosures, subject-to purchases and many others.

His *AIM* system, which stands for **A**ccelerated **I**ncome **M**odel, will empower anyone, regardless of their experience, age, sex, financial condition or even bad credit, to create a life of their dreams.

Creative Real Estate Coaching.
4 Days

In the *Creative Real Estate Coaching* live event and program you will be coached and mentored by master real estate investor Rick C. Ernst on an ongoing basis through a comprehensive *3-tier learning format* consisting of *live events, telephone coaching and email support.*

First tier: Live Event - Two Day Roundtable

As a participant in this coaching program, two times per year you will have the opportunity to attend the two-day roundtable in the vacation capital of the world, beautiful Orlando, Florida. During this event you will receive LIVE training, coaching and support from Rick C. Ernst and other instructors. These live events deliver the latest and most up-to-date creative real estate investing information and techniques allowing you to maintain your cutting edge as a current creative real estate investor.

Second tier: Creative Real Estate Q & A Call.

As a coaching client, you will have the opportunity to bring your real estate deals directly to Rick C. Ernst for LIVE expert coaching. This way you can make sure, you are doing exactly what you need to do to get the deal done right and make the most profit on every real estate transaction.

Third tier: Real Estate Q & A - Email Hotline

Once again, as a coaching client now you can get expert help when you need it, by emailing your real estate buying or selling questions and receiving a quick answer no more than one business day later. This Real Estate email hotline will give you the professional assistance you need to nail down those tough deals. With the experience, expertise and coaching of the Rick C. Ernst *Q & A Hotline* you are sure to get many real estate deals you otherwise might have missed.

Secrets To Luxury Travel
2 Days

At the *Secrets To Luxury Travel event,* you will be lead step-by-step through a comprehensive money saving travel program that will provide you with the knowledge, training and tools necessary to give you direct access to the best travel discounts and benefits available anywhere, any time.

Having access to this exclusive travel discount program will serve all your worldwide personal and/or business travel needs and fulfill all your vacation fantasies.

During this event, you learn how to take full advantage of drastically reduced travel prices and rates. These include:

- Exotic vacation packages
- *Resorts*
- *Hotels*
- *Cruise lines*
- *Air fares,*
- *Car, Motorcycles and RV's rentals*

These are all accessible right from the comfort of your home. One of the most popular benefits is having direct access to worldwide networks of discounted travel connections, which provide *luxury Resort Condominium Accommodations* at lower than standard hotel prices!

At this one-of-a-kind two-day event, you will discover the exciting insider secrets to luxury travel that will benefit you and your loved ones for years to come.

Ultimate Mastery Summit
5 Days

The *Ultimate Mastery Summit* curriculum will maximize your *personal power* and help you to create and master the life you desire. While you enjoy the luxurious accommodations and beautiful Caribbean beaches as well as a state-of-the-art spa and wellness center, you will receive the invaluable benefits of this life-changing program, which is based on the most up-to-date excellent teachings of specialized life experts, scholars, doctors, financial planners and legal and tax experts.

During the 5-days of the *Ultimate Mastery Summit,* you will receive information and tools you need to take the authentic actions that will give each area of your life true meaning and relevance through practical, hands on techniques.

You will learn the proven secrets of gaining mastery of the seven most important areas of your life:

- *Health, Nutrition and Wellness*
- *Feelings, Emotions and Self Expression*
- *Personal and Professional Relationships*
- *Career Fruition, Living Your Life's Passion*
- *Time Segregation and Management*
- *Finance and Wealth Preservation*
- *Spirituality Maturity and Stewardship*

The *Ultimate Mastery Summit* will empower you to totally take charge and actually master your entire life. Enroll now and discover how to master your life from the concepts, principles and wisdom of many of the world's greatest minds.

Due to the individual attention, each participant receives at the *Ultimate Mastery Summit* each event is limited to the first one hundred people who register. If the next event is sold out, you may request to be added to our waiting list.

~

For More Information On
All Of The Above Events Call:

1-888-238-1144

Ask For Extension 1555.

For Complete Details Logon To:

www.MyRicherLife.com

Complimentary
Richer Life Experience Certificate
Value $3,000

The Richer Life Connection and Rick C. Ernst invite you and one family member to attend the Richer Life Experience as complimentary guests. For more information and registration logon to:

www.MyRicherLife.com

If you **cannot** register online, call toll-free:

1-888-238-1144 ask for extension 1555*

When registering use Reference # _____

If there is no above *Reference* number simply leave blank when registering for the event.

---

* This is a *limited time offer* and all complimentary participants must attend the event by the date shown on the website:

www.MyRicherLife.com

This offer is open to all purchasers of *Richer Life Secrets by Rick C. Ernst*. Original proof of purchase is required. The above offer is limited to the Richer Life Experience only and complimentary registration for the event is subject to availability of space and/or changes to event schedule. The value of this complimentary admission for you and a companion is $3,000. To take advantage of this limited time offer you will be required to provide details of a valid credit card for a $100 deposit to secure each seat for the event registration date that you request.

If you do not attend the Richer Life Experience for the date you registered, the $100 deposit will be charged in full for each seat you registered that is not used. To avoid being charged the deposit, cancellations or rescheduling requests must be made at least five (5) business days prior to the commencement of the Richer Life Experience by calling **1-888-238-1144 ask for extension 1555**.

Corporate or organizational purchasers may not use one book to invite more than two people. While complimentary participants are responsible for their travel and other costs, admission to the Richer Life Experience is complimentary. Participants in the event are under no additional financial obligation to the Richer Life Connection or Rick C. Ernst. The Richer Life Connection reserves the right to refuse admission to or remove anyone from the premises it believes is disrupting or may disrupt the event.